HOUSES *of* THE LAKE DISTRICT

'Is the dome by Inigo Jones, too? It looks later.'

'Oh, Charles, don't be such a tourist. What does it matter when it was built, if it's pretty?'

'It's the sort of thing I like to know.'

'Oh dear, I thought I'd cured you of all that – the terrible Mr Collins.'

It was an aesthetic education to live within those walls, to wander from room to room, from the Soanesque library to the Chinese drawing-room, adazzle with gilt pagodas and nodding mandarins, painted paper and Chippendale fretwork, from the Pompeian parlour to the great tapestry-hung hall which stood unchanged, as it had been designed two hundred and fifty years before; to sit, hour after hour, in the shade looking out on the terrace.

Evelyn Waugh, *Brideshead Revisited*

HOUSES *of*
THE LAKE
DISTRICT

Christopher Holliday
Photographs by Clive Boursnell

F

FRANCES LINCOLN LIMITED
PUBLISHERS

Frances Lincoln Limited
4 Torriano Mews
Torriano Avenue
London NW5 2RZ
www.franceslincoln.com

ENDPAPERS
FRONT Troutbeck Park Farm, donated by Beatrix Potter to the National Trust.
BACK The Kent Estuary, looking towards Arnside Knott, the southern boundary of Cumbria.

PAGE 1: Wordsworth House, Cockermouth, where William Wordsworth was born in 1770. He shared this bedroom with his siblings, Richard, Dorothy, John and Christopher.
PAGES 2–3: Helm Crag, 'the Lion and the Lamb', Grasmere, an inspiration to Wordsworth while he lived at Dove Cottage.
RIGHT Georgian gazebo in the garden at Dalemain, Ullswater.

CONTENTS

INTRODUCTION

Although most visitors think of Cumbria in terms of romantic scenery – perhaps the most remarkable scenery in England – and picturesque natural landscape, the county also boasts a fine stock of distinguished houses and castles. This book is about some of the best of these.

All the houses are open to visitors. Many of the castles and country houses are still inhabited by the same family after numerous generations, and are open to the public as family homes with a warm welcome considered the priority. Other houses are owned by trusts that do everything possible to make a visit a tangible and meaningful experience. The book devotes itself to surviving castles and houses with their roofs still on, their fixtures and fittings largely intact; ruined castles such as Brough and Brougham are not included, as they are another subject in themselves.

These are not the great houses of England, the seats of power associated with the country's greatest landowners. They were not designed to dazzle in the manner of Blenheim in Oxfordshire and Chatsworth in Derbyshire; nor are they treasure houses on the scale of Harewood in Yorkshire or Woburn in Bedfordshire. The historic dwellings to be found within these pages are of note not least because they are located in some of the most breathtaking scenery in England, and inextricably linked with their settings, but also for other reasons.

First, it is fascinating to observe how each house speaks of the comfort of the age in which it was built. Its architectural style is often a display of charm and personality, revealing much of the way of life of the times when it was created and the people who lived there.

Second, social changes often bypassed this part of the country. Living in a county remote from London and the

Stoney Lane, Near Sawrey, from Hill Top, which Beatrix Potter purchased in 1905.

The kitchen at Townend.

clamour of changing fashion, where arable farming was a struggle but where wool was the oil of its day, conservative owners felt secure and did not make fashion a priority. Sometimes decades would pass when a house was not considered the owner's main home, as was the case with Levens Hall. Occasionally frugality or inertia led owners to allow their houses to be bypassed by architectural fashion. Sometimes a family would fall on hard times, incur debts and be forced to curtail its activities. All these reasons helped to ensure that in several of these houses time stood still; Levens Hall and much of Sizergh Castle have hardly been altered. Domestic houses such as Swarthmoor Hall and Townend have also survived the centuries with some alterations but not enough to change the character of the place.

Third, the Lake District has as rich a literary seam running through it as any county in England, and fame has sometimes been thrust upon a house because of its association with a writer, thus making it unique. The houses lived in by, or associated with, William Wordsworth, John Ruskin and Beatrix Potter, who all loved and championed the Lakes, have survived intact and are all open to view, largely as their incumbents would have known them. Popular today because of that notoriety, they also provide a link with the past and reveal some of the idiosyncrasies of domestic architecture. These authors' celebration and protection of the Lake District offer another strand to the history of these remarkable houses. All three writers recognized the importance of preserving what visitors were coming to enjoy and were influential in preventing overdevelopment in the central area of Cumbria that became the Lake

Dalemain: one of several Cumbrian houses built around a pele tower.

District National Park in 1951. (Cumbria was created in 1974 when the government's county reorganization joined Cumberland, Westmorland and Lancashire north-of-the-sands. Cumbria is England's second largest county, after north Yorkshire, extending to over 6,475 square kilometres/2,500 square miles. The Lake District National Park, which extends to almost 2,330 square kilometres/900 square miles contained within Cumbria, is usually referred to as the Lake District or Lakeland.)

The houses are presented here in broadly chronological order, focusing on the period that represents the house best. If a house was built, say, eight hundred years ago but was later remodelled in the fashion of a particular period, it is placed in the chronology of the period from which most of the property dates – as in the case of Holker, which is primarily a Victorian remodelling of an older house, or Hutton-in-the-Forest, in which, though it spans six different centuries, the Victorian overlay on the house is dominant.

Many of the houses and castles – such as Dalemain and Muncaster Castle – have a pele tower as their central core. Pele towers were Cumbria's greatest defence, built to ward off the Scots and strategically placed on the county's long borders.

As Cumbria was England's most north-westerly county, bordering Scotland, it has a long, harsh history of being under threat from the Scots, from as long ago as the Roman occupation (AD 43–410). In particular, it had to endure frequent Scottish raids from the twelfth century to the second half of the fourteenth century. 'The debatable land' of the Borders, as it was known,

The pele tower at Isel Hall, Cockermouth. The pink finish is an authentic colour of the period.

was far removed from the power bases of the English and Scottish monarchs, so lawlessness went unchallenged; fire and sword were part of everyday Cumbrian life. Scottish raiders slaughtered villagers, burned towns and desecrated churches. In addition Border reivers from either side, with allegiance only to their own clans, plundered and pillaged in cross-border raids. Small bands of ten to twenty men would regularly swoop down on each other's territory for bouts of cattle rustling and pillaging, creating an atmosphere of permanent crisis steeped in robbery, extortion, kidnap and murder. For several centuries those who lived in the Borders had a precarious life, akin almost to that in America's 'Wild West' of the nineteenth century.

To combat these raids, landowners needed to fortify their properties. Impregnability was all. The most common defence was the stone Norman fortified keep; the fortified style of Cumbria's castles owes much to these early border defences, and castle keeps are prevalent in this part of the world. The keep evolved into the tower house or pele tower. By the middle of the fourteenth century these defensive pele towers, built by the barons and influential families, were appearing on both sides of the border.

From the outside a pele tower's appearance is that of a square squat tower, roughly 18 metres/60 feet high and 12.25 metres/40 feet wide. Key defence features include walls up to 3 metres/10 feet thick, small windows and the roof being hidden behind battlements. The building materials were often rough rubble masonry, but if better stone was available it would be dressed as smoothed ashlar, jointed and built in regular blocks. The two most frequently found types of stone, limestone and sandstone, lent themselves to being cut and carved, but sandstone is prone to vicious weathering.

In such a strong refuge – a year-round residence with accommodation for animals, standing within a protective stockade – a family could feel relatively secure. Shelter would be extended to the local people whenever a raid was threatened. The ground floor was the most vulnerable area, so this tunnel-vaulted room was often used to safeguard livestock and for storage. The family would live in the unpartitioned storey above. Known as the solar, as it was a light room, this was the principal apartment. The sleeping quarters could be found in the floor above, the top storey. The design of the tower with a few slit windows and a parapet allowed the occupants to defend themselves.

The bloody feuding persisted between the Scots and English until the union of England and Scotland with the accession of James I of England (James VI of Scotland) in 1603. Border strife finally petered out with the Act of Union in 1707.

Pele towers still survive, stretching between the west and east coasts. Some, such as Kentmere Hall near Kendal, are used for agricultural purposes. Some are now part of a great house, for once the need for defence was less imperative, and as times grew safer and more peaceful, the pele lived on, not as a place of retreat but as the core of subsequent extensions. At Levens Hall after 1580, the mid-fourteenth-century pele tower and hall were converted into a gentleman's residence. Other pele towers were embellished, as we shall see.

Sizergh Castle retains its fourteenth-century pele tower and, like Levens, is predominantly Elizabethan. Elizabethan houses exude grandeur and an infectious *joie de vivre*. The wealthiest aristocrats could afford to revel in elaborate ornamentation, and their red-brick houses with splendid windows and fantastical arrangements of spiralling chimneys reveal a great deal about the spirit of the age.

Two fine examples of the smaller Elizabethan house have also survived: Swarthmoor Hall, the birthplace of the Quaker movement, and Townend, a late sixteenth- or early seventeenth-century Lakeland yeoman's farmhouse near Windermere. Both houses retain the roughcast finish that dresses those old whitewashed or limewashed stone cottages to be found in picture-postcard Lakeland towns and villages. The roughcast looks appealing when limewashed or painted, but its main purpose is to prevent the lashing rain from seeping between the stones. Limewashed roughcast walls are among those familiar seventeenth-century Cumbrian features, such as steep Westmorland green slate roofs, irregular gables, cylindrical chimneys and mullioned windows set flush with the façades, that have continued to inspire architects working in the region ever since.

To Hutton-in-the-Forest's pele tower two new wings were added in the seventeenth century. In the Jacobean era the family built a Renaissance gallery and cloister, which were followed towards the end of the seventeenth century by a new front and entrance. Georgian additions comprised a suite of three delightful rooms, including a small drawing room and two bedrooms. A remarkable building emerged and it was further embellished with a grand tower by the late Georgians. Later still, Hutton was refurbished in the mid-Victorian medieval revival style.

Unlike the arable south with its agrarian revolution of the 1530s, partly because of its remoteness and the mountainous landscape, Cumbria was not affected by the Agricultural Revolution until the late seventeenth and early eighteenth centuries. This period saw the rebuilding of wooden houses in stone, and drystone walls began appearing around 1750, acting as enclosures on land to be used to feed a growing urban population. The Enclosure Acts worked in the Lakes: as the Napoleonic Wars of 1793–1815 made it harder to import and food prices were rising at the time, it paid farmers to reclaim wasteland and commons. Mining created new prosperity. Lead and copper mining had been long established in Cumbria, but coal mining in the west around Whitehaven, lead mining in the north Pennines around Alston Moor and the largest steelworks in the world at Barrow-in-Furness all demonstrate that the Industrial Revolution did not pass the county by. The scores of rivers and becks were also pressed into service, to power the making of bobbins for the mills of Lancashire, wood hurdles in Yorkshire and cloth in Carlisle.

Dalemain reigns supreme as the finest example of an eighteenth-century country house in the county. The combined jumble of a pele tower and rambling Tudor wings made it difficult to impose Georgian symmetry, but the problem was solved by building a new façade and effectively making these disappear; from the front it is hard to believe that such balance and symmetry conceal a pele tower and great hall.

In the nineteenth century, the first squeakings of the gothic revival in Cumbria appeared in 1821 when building started on Conishead Priory, near Ulverston, a riotously ambitious house that defies pigeonholing. The Victorian medieval revival was fuelled by the locations and style of the more romantic dwellings, such as Muncaster Castle, located on a promontory on Cumbria's west coast, and Anthony Salvin's inspirational treatments of Muncaster Castle and Hutton-in-the-Forest in the 1860s are triumphant examples of high Victorian revelry.

At Hutton Salvin designed a south-east tower and south elevation and the major reception rooms between 1860 and 1880. Muncaster Castle was his largest commission in Cumbria. He largely rebuilt it in the neo-medieval style in 1862 and that is what we see today. Its most glorious room is the library, a double-storey octagon soaring to a gothic vault, while elsewhere in the castle Salvin was inspired to create a barrel-vaulted drawing room, a dining room clad in leather embossed with gold leaf and a fine great hall complete with heraldic windows and wood carving.

The library at Muncaster Castle, designed by the architect Anthony Salvin.

Salvin's work is eclipsed only by the opulent treatment of Holker Hall's new wing in the 1870s. Holker Hall stands alone as a sumptuous Victorian rebuild of a wing razed to the ground by fire in 1871. It is one of several houses once owned by the Dukes of Devonshire and the sumptuous 'new' wing designed to lavish ducal specifications is open to visitors today. The Lancaster architects Paley & Austin presented the 7th Duke with a thrilling Elizabethan revival which almost dwarfs the original Jacobean wing and boasts a cupola and a square tower reminiscent of a pele, a double-storey circular bay, a riot of chimneys and a multitude of gables. It is a remarkable achievement. The wing celebrates the pioneering spirit of both centuries: the Elizabethan grand manner reminds us of that confident age, yet the wing is unmistakably Victorian. With all the late Victorian sophistication that the interior decorator firm of J.G. Crace could muster, Holker's interiors are warmer and more feminine than the style found in houses built in tougher times. A drawing room lined with Macclesfield silk, a hand-stencilled billiard room of the richest green and sumptuous bedrooms all help to make this one of the county's most charismatic houses.

Meanwhile, much was changing in Cumbria as a result of the coming of the railways. Carlisle became connected to Newcastle in 1838, and the line was followed in the 1840s by one cutting through the Lune Gorge and over Shap Summit (278 metres/914 feet) before reaching Carlisle. The railway significantly aided industrial activity and gave the tourist industry a great boost.

Until the late eighteenth century, Cumberland and Westmorland were remote and cut off. The route across Morecambe Bay between Lancaster and Cartmel Priory was a familiar one for travellers with a purpose, but otherwise the area remained inaccessible and the mountains forbidding and difficult to negotiate. This was not an area you chose to visit unless you had to.

Gradually all this began to alter. Turnpike roads were improved in the middle of the eighteenth century and these encouraged the first travellers to the area. Because of war in Europe, England

The library at Holker Hall, designed by Lancaster architects Paley & Austin.

became the place for the Grand Tour in its stead. Writers such as the poet Thomas Gray, who wrote about the Lake District in 1769, began to ignite travellers' imaginations and encourage interest in the Picturesque. Many would arrive clutching their copy of Father Thomas West's *A Guide to the Lakes*, published in 1778. Gilpin's two volumes of *Observations, On Several Parts Of England, Particularly The Mountains And Lakes Of Cumberland And Westmorland, Relative Chiefly To Picturesque Beauty* of 1792 and 1808 led the way to the building of houses located to enjoy the site and the views. Wordsworth's best-selling *Guide to the Lakes* of 1810 and 1835, and in 1855 Harriet Martineau's *Complete Guide to the Lakes*, further encouraged visitors.

With the coming of the branch line to Windermere in 1847 mass tourism in the central Lakes began, although there was extreme opposition to it. Wordsworth, for one, was seriously afraid of hordes of common Lancashire people descending on Lakeland and, worse for him, venturing into his home vale of Grasmere. As if airbrushing away the inspiration of his early poems in which he had elevated the poor, and ignoring the impact of his *Guide to the Lakes*, he fired off letters to newspapers, appealed to Gladstone and left no doubt as to his state of mind in 'Railway', composed in 1844, in which he wrote: 'Is then no nook of English ground secure/From rash assault?' Meanwhile he sent his agent to buy shares in the railway. Though the opposition was not wholly successful, it prevented the line from continuing as far as Grasmere and Rydal.

When the railway to Windermere was eventually completed in 1847, the once peaceful surroundings were altered for ever. The trickle of visitors that had started when the Picturesque notion of the Lake District was 'discovered' in the late eighteenth century became a roaring tumult. After disembarking from the train at Windermere visitors could easily reach the immediate surroundings with a short carriage drive. The new town of Windermere, formerly the village of Birthwaite, was centred on the railway station, and was a mile north of the small village of Bowness-on-Windermere, which hastily beefed itself up and became a resort.

The railway not only revolutionized travel for the masses but also brought a different type of wealth to the area. Some of the major industrialists from the north-west – mill owners and brewing and distillery families, who had long been visiting the Lakes for holidays – were suddenly in a position to build their own villas and mansions to rival those of the aristocracy. Not only did this new wealthy class seek spiritual refreshment in the Lake District: they wished to escape the threat of disease rife in the heat of summer in the cities where they had amassed their fortunes. From the middle of the nineteenth century they began to make their increasingly regular holidays in pursuit of the Picturesque rather more permanent. Around the northern shores of Windermere they built grandiose and spacious houses and stuccoed villas – some inspired by the outward appearance of the square pele tower – in prime locations of waterside settings with fine views across the lake towards the Langdale Pikes and glorious sunsets. Blackwell, an Arts and Crafts house of 1898–1900, built as a holiday home for Sir Edward Holt, a Manchester brewer and philanthropist, is one of these.

The new building by Victorian grandees continued until the beginning of the twentieth century. Fortunately, though, by the turn of the century the building development had peaked. The area has never been exploited to the extent of some of the European lakes and resorts enjoying similarly inspirational scenery and, notwithstanding the large concentrations of population less than two hours' drive away, the Lake District has remained largely unspoilt by developers. Lacking similar easy access by rail, and a short carriage drive to your mansion, the area along the western shore around Hawkshead has remained far less developed, with the various villages and hamlets remaining small.

At the time, though, these new ostentatious buildings were regarded as something of an invasion, fuelling the campaign against the overdevelopment of the Lakes. So it is no coincidence that the Lake District was the birthplace of a new charity known as the National Trust in 1895. This was formed to 'look after places of historic interest or natural beauty permanently for the benefit of the nation across England, Wales and Northern Ireland'. Most importantly, the trust 'has the unique statutory power to declare land inalienable'. The acquisition of Brandelhow Park on Derwentwater in 1902 was its first in England and Wales. The National Trust benefited hugely from Beatrix Potter's love of the area when she left 4,000 acres and 14 farms to it on her death in 1943. It looks after a quarter of the Lake District National Park.

Intrusions they might have been, but Windermere's Victorian villas and mansions represent something of a golden era, which vanished after the First World War. Built for an age of servants, hardly any of these houses have survived as private houses run on Victorian lines, but many of them have been put to good use and have tapped into the visitor market as hotels with well-preserved reception rooms. Others have been converted into apartments. Many are situated near or overlooking the lakes and fells, affording splendid opportunities to enjoy fine views from within; waterside reflections and borrowed landscape enhance the setting from outside. A lake cruise affords the best view of them. Occasionally the main house has become a footnote,

View of the Langdale Pikes with the setting sun from Langdale Chase on the north-eastern shore of Windermere.

dwarfed by bedroom and dining-room extensions, but most have been sensitively extended to the rear, which faces the road, and in spite of various extensions the original building is usually still recognizable. From the lake at any rate there is still a reminder of the *belle époque*.

Four of the grand houses that have survived around Windermere and which can be viewed are Broad Leys, Langdale Chase, Blackwell and Wray Castle. Broad Leys is owned by the Windermere Motor Boat Racing Club; Langdale Chase has been a prestigious hotel for many decades now; Blackwell is open to the public; Wray Castle is owned by the National Trust and is due to be converted into a hotel. Only Langdale Chase has been extended.

After the First and Second World Wars the world of the country house changed irrevocably. Scores of magnificent houses in the United Kingdom became social anachronisms and were demolished, but the Lakes counties have fared well. There have been casualties such as Lowther Castle, roofless since the 1950s, but many country houses survive, and remain in remarkably full possession of their contents.

Integral to the charm of the houses are their gardens, their characteristics determined by the varied topography of the area. Apart from the fells, which create drama and provide shelter, and the lakes offering tranquil reflections, Cumbria has a long expanse of coastline extending north from Arnside to just south of Gretna Green on the Scottish border. Its location as a northerly outpost creates a harsh and unforgiving image, but it has many advantages. The western seaboard enjoys ample rainfall – the prevailing westerly wind blowing in from the Atlantic brings copious amounts of water with it – and, apart from occasional long dry spells, as in 2010

The topiary at Levens Hall, dating back to 1694.

(when there was minimal rainfall for three months from April to the end of June), there is rarely a summer week without some rain; there is little call for drought-tolerant gardening. The Lake District soil is often full of stones, with rock not far below the surface, but what earth there is rarely dries out because of the usual regular rainfall. Normally the excellent drainage provided by the stones prevents the land from becoming waterlogged, which is particularly important in winter, when favourite garden stalwarts from the Mediterranean such as lavender cannot cope with their roots sitting in water.

The Lake District's rugged landscape demands appropriate gardening for the location. There are not many parterres perched on hillsides, but terraces retain the earth and provide level areas for borders and paths. Changes of level usually make a garden much more interesting, as the visitor is seldom able to see the garden all at once. On the other hand, Cumbria's level gardens, such as that at Levens Hall, show how hedges can divide space into different 'rooms' so that the garden cannot be seen at one glance. And in Levens the county can boast the world's most famous topiary garden, dating from 1694. Here once again the county being so far from London has paid dividends. Thanks to owners feeling there was little urgency to fall over themselves in pursuit of the latest fads, the topiary garden survived unscathed and now after decades in the fashion wilderness it has come into its own, emerging as a rare example of an all but forgotten style of gardening.

This is woodland and fern country, and only the occasional drought turns the fells brown and makes the bracken, gorse and peat tinder dry by autumn. The west coast often has milder winters than inland counties and the east coast, so there is ample opportunity to echo the lush plantings of Cornwall. Big-leaved evergreens such as rhododendrons flourish. Valleys provide shelter and the fells protect

The gardens at Muncaster Castle.

them from battering winds, but on this side of the country the wind seldom comes rampaging over from Russia and the Continent, tearing at everything in its wake.

The western seaboard rainfall, which keeps the lakes and rivers full, combined with acid soil, inspired late nineteenth-century plantsmen to cultivate the azaleas, rhododendrons and Japanese maples for which the county is famous. These small-rooted plants never expect to seek out moisture and are used to ample rainfall, so are well suited to the area. With a backdrop of fell and ravine these plants look very much at home, in some respects almost Himalayan. On the west coast the gardens of Muncaster Castle support what was once the largest collection of rhododendrons in Europe, hundreds of which have grown to a prodigious size. Almost touching Morecambe Bay in the south, Holker Hall also has some magnificent rhododendrons within a sloping woodland setting. Likewise the extensive woodland garden at Mirehouse and Wordsworth's plantings at Rydal Mount are in harmony with the surrounding woodland and water.

Although many gardens are favoured by the mild coastal climate, conditions are colder in the north of the county and gardens located on higher ground are more exposed. In those gardens where big-leaved evergreens such as rhododendrons are likely to struggle, gardens usually excel at herbaceous borders. Dalemain and Hutton-in-the-Forest, both near Penrith, rely on fine formal perennial gardens sheltering beneath sturdy walls. The usually reliable summer rainfall helps borders to shrug off that tired look from which gardens in warmer and drier counties can suffer; they often improve, as Scottish herbaceous borders do.

The gardens have also benefited from the interest of keen gardeners such as Wordsworth, a passionate plantsman and designer, and Ruskin, who was something of an experimenter.

Although the once familiar image of a country house as a private family home running on Edwardian lines like a well-oiled machine has now gone for ever, this kind of house and the others described in this book are a key part of our heritage and still have an essential role to play today. Society needs space to relax and unwind, and as space in the countryside decreases, with urban sprawl and a growing population, there is more pressure on the countryside and its many attractions. Visiting houses, estates, parks and gardens has therefore become more popular than ever; visits have escalated dramatically in recent years, as people have realized that an admission ticket represents a day out of remarkably good value, especially as the larger houses have enough interest to inspire visitors for a full day and most have superb attractions for children of all ages.

In turn, the houses need visitors. Many of the large country houses across Britain have not retained the acreages of land they once possessed and have therefore lost revenue they could rely upon from tenants. Keeping a house in order continues to be an enormous responsibility: ageing houses require constant maintenance and have become increasingly expensive to run, especially when legislation demands that time-honoured procedures which are often labour intensive are used. The loss of revenue from tenants and these spiralling costs combine to make it imperative for house owners and trusts (apart from those that are now hotels) to seek innovative ways of generating further income. Unless the house has other financial interests and investments, the number of visitors a house welcomes every year is often the key to its survival.

Presentation is everything and over the years historic houses have become far more inventive about how they present themselves. Look no further than the streamlined country house websites with their shifting wide-angle photographs. The Ealing comedy days of *Kind Hearts and Coronets* with a superior owner mustering all his airs and graces while collecting the shillings from the visitors have long gone. Owners and trusts have had to become far more commercially aware, managing what is essentially a family business themselves or employing professionals to do so.

Although some houses stay open almost the whole year round, the seasonal nature of the business means that there is a window of only a few prime months in which to draw the crowds, with the highest visitor numbers determined by school holidays. But the summer is not necessarily a guarantee of high numbers: if it is excessively wet or too warm people stay at home. Many British families jet off abroad for their main holiday, so this cuts the number of potential visitors during the summer, though foreign tourists offset this to some extent.

But the houses of the Lake District are perhaps more fortunate than houses in other parts of the country. We have seen that, rather like Venice, the Lake District is an old hand at welcoming visitors, having done so since the eighteenth century, and as each year goes by they arrive in increasing numbers. Although the Lake District has always been somewhat remote, which is one of its charms, it is not much more than an hour's drive from much of Lancashire and Yorkshire. Whether for a day excursion, a weekend away or a major holiday, the Lake District enthrals millions of visitors a year. When people plan a break in the Lake District, they usually take a broad overview of the area. The Lakeland scenery is an obvious draw, and most visitors' prime reason for making a visit. But so too are the attractive towns and villages, and historic sites such as castles, ruins, notable churches and places of interest such as houses and gardens. The ample rainfall that keeps the streams and lakes full and the fellsides green is an asset; when the rain descends, the car park queues for indoor visitor attractions lengthen.

A house's location within the Lake District can make an enormous difference to its visitor numbers. Those properties within easy reach of the central Lake District have a guaranteed audience. Dove Cottage in Grasmere, open since 1891, is an example; Wordsworth is one of the nation's best-loved poets, with a dedicated international following. Much the same can be said of Beatrix Potter. The National Trust hardly needs to promote her home, such is its

overwhelming popularity. The fabric of the small building and its contents are at risk under the strain of numbers; timed tickets in high season have become the norm.

Those houses further afield, such as Muncaster Castle on the west coast, have more of a fight on their hands. Accordingly they feel compelled to organize a wide-ranging seasonal programme of events to entice visitors to go that extra mile. It is not a difficult journey to Muncaster – indeed it is a highly enjoyable scenic drive – but the west coast just takes that bit longer to reach. Other houses on the edge of the county know that innovation is often born of necessity; some of them astonish with their resourcefulness. Who would associate Elizabethan Levens Hall with an annual chilli fest? How did Jane Hasell-McCosh at Dalemain anticipate that a marmalade competition could take off in mid-winter?

Wherever its location, most houses must work hard to attract new visitors, maintain the public's interest and keep the interest going so as to attract visitors on more than one occasion. There are two main markets to which they must appeal: the local population and those from further afield who will make a one-off visit on a day trip or as part of their holiday. Annual season tickets and friends' schemes create loyalty and a family feeling.

The visiting public's thirst for novelty also has to be recognized. When you have a house several hundred years old, the suggestion that there is nothing fresh to say about it has to be stifled. The owners or custodians realize that a house needs to be reinvented to some extent with special exhibitions; a flourishing programme of events taking place in a vibrant environment strikes a positive note.

Most houses have organized themselves so that there are plenty of extra areas of interest and points of sale. As well as coming to see the house and garden, visitors who arrive on a normal opening day are entertained with tempting cuisine and gifts from a specialist shop. Occasionally the visit to the actual property seems almost forgotten in the fray of additional activities available. If you visit most of the country houses in the UK that open on a bank holiday or when there is a special event in the grounds, the chances are the interior will be deserted, while the café, shop and playground will be under siege. After all, the British can never turn from a cup of tea when they start to flag, and if they discover that perfect scone, jam and cream they will remember the day for ever. There is a growing enthusiasm for high-quality locally sourced produce from an

estate. The recent addition of Holker Hall's food hall has been very successful. Garden shops selling plants are always a winner.

Today's children are tomorrow's visitors, so most houses encourage school trips and educational days out. Schools are encouraged to make return visits, with many estates offering multiple subjects to study. Live interpretations, children's activity packs, face-painting and hands-on activities beckon even the most uninterested of nine-year-olds. In addition mazes, children's play areas, quizzes and trails, guides especially for children, Easter Egg trails, Hallowe'en and Christmas grottos all jostle for attention. Volunteers wearing historic costumes bring the past alive and make it more identifiable.

Even so, although visitors are a welcome and valuable source of revenue, increasing the numbers year on year is difficult if the owners are not to spoil the very atmosphere and tranquillity of the house that they have come to enjoy. Holding special events has the advantage that the house itself is not threatened with too much extra traffic, yet continues to present a vibrant and upbeat image. Special events, especially those held in the open, have been a salvation in the last decade or so, helping to reignite interest during the season. Theatre performances and concerts in the park keep the gates open during evenings, when they would normally shut. Corporate events and private bookings are also valuable sources of income, and the ability to host civil wedding ceremonies has been an enormous boost, although some properties decline the opportunity for fear of damage.

The scale and variety of events organized by these houses is enormous. They reveal a desire to reinvent, to move with the times and to maintain the interest in a house without the visitor experience becoming static. It is often said that every time you return to a house or garden you always see something new that you missed on a previous occasion.

In addition to performing a good deed, a charity event raises a house's profile. The National Gardens Scheme (NGS) raises money primarily for charities in the caring and nursing sectors and enlists both public and private gardens to open for at least one day for a year in aid of its charities. Several properties such as Conishead Priory, Holker Hall, Hutton-in-the-Forest and Sizergh Castle all open for at least a day in aid of the NGS. Hutton-in-the-Forest also opens for the British Red Cross on specified dates. Holker Hall runs a series of fund-raising events under the direction of Lady Cavendish, with concerts and suppers in support of the local hospice, Riding for the Disabled and the NSPCC.

Those who are responsible for the houses in this book work hard to attract visitors to them. Some – like the present owners of Levens Hall, Dalemain, Hutton-in-the-Forest, Muncaster Castle and Holker Hall, who can all look back on two or more decades of continuous stewardship of great distinction – do so in order to keep the house in their family and pass it on to the generation who follow them. They have a deep love and respect for their family home, a strong sense of history and a keen awareness that they provide local employment; and, although the traditional use of their home has changed to that of visitor attraction, they would fight tooth and nail to keep the whole enterprise flourishing. Private owners or custodians alike maintain these remarkable houses as part of our heritage, and because of their beauty, history and interest.

HISTORIC HOUSES

SIZERGH CASTLE

'Ancestral voices prophesying war!'

S izergh Castle, near Kendal, has a baffling exterior until you realize that the house is a collection of buildings and extensions spanning several different periods. The core of the castle is a fourteenth-century pele tower surrounded by a Tudor house. In Elizabethan times the castle was given a major overhaul to enlarge it and make it more comfortable, but thereafter lack of fortune restrained the family from pursuing new fashions and, apart from having a Georgian drawing room added, it has remained largely untouched ever since.

The west front and its carriage entrance is a good place to start when considering the castle's history. Ignoring the two Elizabethan wings flanking the courtyard for the moment, let us concentrate on the central range. This is the medieval part of the castle, most of which has been overlaid at a later date.

The oldest section on the right-hand side is the mid-fourteenth-century square tower, which has hardly changed. The limestone rubble walls vary in thickness, being 2.3–2.9 metres/7½–9½ feet at ground level and gradually decreasing in width as the walls become higher, to four-storey height. The tower provided the family's most frequented apartment, the solar, located on the first floor out of harm's way; this was effectively their living room. The Deincourt Tower is slightly taller and contains the staircase. The coat of arms, also mid-fourteenth century, below the highest window celebrates the union of Deincourt and Strickland families in 1239.

The central section immediately to the left of this tower dates from the mid-1550s, when the castle evolved from medieval hall into an Elizabethan house. This Elizabethan enlargement once had three gables, but these were replaced by the battlemented roof and walls studded with gothic windows by the architect John Hird of Cartmel, dating from 1773–4. The main entrance used to be via a flight of external steps leading to a first-floor door, now replaced by the final addition to the castle, the gothic carriage entrance, completed in 1902. This is wide enough for a coach and four to drive through to the east side.

PREVIOUS PAGES An Elizabethan plaster ceiling in the Great Hall at Levens.
LEFT Sizergh Castle's castellated pele tower, with the Deincourt Tower thrusting outwards.

LEFT ABOVE The mid-fourteenth-century coat of arms on the pele tower shows the union of the Deincourt and Strickland families in 1239.
LEFT BELOW An Elizabethan barge board on the kitchen wing.
ABOVE The Elizabethan gable, the castellated Georgian central section and the fourteenth-century pele tower (seen from left to right) demonstrate Sizergh's many transformations.

The left-hand single gable also dates from the mid-1550s. Originally this wing provided additional apartments and heightened the medieval service block. The early Georgian sash windows at first-floor level are the only changes here. The wing has since been pushed to the sidelines by the more imposing central battlemented section.

The two wings flanking the courtyard comprise the north wing to the left and the south wing to the right. The north wing provided accommodation for the servants and housed the kitchen. The exterior chimneystack is as wide as a house and can be viewed from the rock garden behind. The jumble of windows from different periods indicates the internal changes that have taken place.

On the south wing, the regular pattern of the windows indicates a long gallery, which was built over 'self-contained lodgings'. The end of this wing now houses a private chapel. This approach to the house is so full of interest that it is easy to miss three pairs of beautifully weathered Elizabethan carved oak bargeboards,.

On the other side of the castle, the east elevation overlooking the lake offers a view of other features of the house from the different building periods. The central section at first-floor level contains the Georgian drawing room, squeezed between the fourteenth-century tower on its left and the gable of the Elizabethan wing on its right. An external staircase leads to a first-floor balcony that runs parallel to the drawing room. The eighteenth-century Venetian windows in the tower on the left and in the Elizabethan wing on the right fit seamlessly. When the stonework was cleaned and repointed in 2009, the operation forced the demise of a mature Virginia creeper that used to colour the tower with its spectacular red autumn tints, but now the beauty of the refurbished stone and the different styles of window can be enjoyed more easily.

When you cross the threshold into what used to be the great medieval hall, you are confronted by a high oak screen of 1558, but beyond this the remains of the medieval hall are soon apparent. The hall would have been a traditional double-storey room where visitors were received. Its lofty height was lost when the Elizabethan great hall was introduced on a new first-floor level in the 1550s and

Walter Strickland (1675–1715) converted what remained of the ground-floor hall into a formal entrance hall. There were further alterations in the 1770s when the Elizabethan hall on the first floor became the drawing room.

The old first-floor entrance door on the west front and the external double flight of steps were swept away in the late nineteenth century to make the carriage porch, the old door becoming a window in the twentieth century. The new entrance allowed the family to be transported into the heart of the building without getting out of their carriage in the open.

Upstairs in the upper hall, or half-landing, a sixteenth-century carved stone doorcase marks the place where steps would once have led from the hall below to the family apartments in the tower.

The banqueting hall on the second floor of the fourteenth-century pele tower, in the space that would have once been the family's main sleeping apartment, gives a wonderful impression of size and scale. The floor above was removed in the middle of the nineteenth century to create a double-storey hall that embraced the romantic medievalism then fashionable. The gallery located at the height of the old floor is anything but medieval, and was fashioned in 1948 from timbers taken from a sixteenth-century barn. The fourteenth-century three-light window is the genuine article, as are the sixteenth-century oak boards.

The dining room gives an insight into the size of the solar, the family's main living area, which would have taken up the whole first floor of the mid-fourteenth-century pele tower. Walter Strickland divided this floor in the 1560s to create the Queen's Room, which incorporates the south-facing end, and the present dining room. This would have been the great chamber, the room that superseded the great hall for formal dining, dancing and games; it then became a drawing room in the mid-eighteenth century for 150 years, eventually becoming the formal dining room in the 1890s.

The dining room's Elizabethan pedigree remains remarkably intact, apart from a late Victorian window introduced to replace a pair of Georgian sash windows. The room is fully panelled, its climax an elaborately carved Italian Renaissance-style overmantel, dated 1564, on which coats of arms of the Strickland family and those connected with them through marriage alliances are displayed amid a riot of foliage and female figures, while male figures bear baskets of fruit. Italian influences come to the fore in the net-like ceiling from a design by Sebastiano Serlio (1475–1554). Serlio was an Italian mannerist architect whose treatises on architecture were intended as illustrated handbooks for architects and were widely influential; he also published several inspirational pattern books, the designs of which were later copied.

Unusually, family portraits are not given pride of place, as is traditional; instead, portraits of the royal House of Stuart are a firm reminder of the family's allegiance at the time: the Strickland family backed the Stuart king James II during his exile in Saint-Germain in France. These portraits were painted in France, and the early eighteenth-century French gilt frames are personalized with the emblems individual to each sitter.

The neo-classical drawing room of 1773–4, by the architect John Hird of Cartmel, is located centrally on the first floor, occupying the space originally created for the Elizabethan great hall out of the upper reaches of the medieval hall. Sweeping changes had to be made to create this room. The fireplace on the long exterior wall disappeared to become a glazed door between new arched windows. On the opposite inner wall a new central doorway and round-headed alcoves achieved the desired symmetry as well as accommodating stoves. Some areas remained only half-plastered and by the 1790s had to be hidden by tapestries. Thirty years later this room had become the billiard room; it did not flower as the drawing room until the early twentieth century.

ABOVE The sixteenth-century stone doorcase between the former great hall and the family apartments.
RIGHT The banqueting hall in the pele tower.

FOLLOWING PAGES
LEFT ABOVE The Elizabethan dining room, located on the first floor of the pele tower in the former solar.
LEFT BELOW The oak-ribbed ceiling of the Queen's Room, inspired by pattern books produced by Sebastiano Serlio.
RIGHT ABOVE The eighteenth-century first-floor drawing room, created from the double-storey great hall.
RIGHT BELOW The overmantel in the dining room. The elaborately carved woodwork in Italian Renaissance style is regarded as being among England's finest carvings.

The National Trust has given the room an eighteenth-century lustre, with blue damask-patterned wallpaper and gold silk damask drapes.

Sizergh's finest and most opulent room is the inlaid chamber. This reveals the importance of an Elizabethan bedroom. The chamber was built around 1575 for Alice Strickland and her third husband, Sir Thomas Boynton, as the state bedroom, reserved for only the most illustrious of guests.

The highlights are the panelling and the ceiling. The inlay of pale poplar contrasted with glossy, dark bog oak above five-panelled framing is considered to be some of the highest craftsmanship in England. The interweaving of the two timbers creates a magnificent jewelled effect, designed to impress the

The inlaid chamber, and (above) its three-sided porch.

visitor. The ceiling is thought to be inspired by the Serlio pattern book. Heraldic beasts such as the goat and stag encased in roundels denote family crests and coats of arms; the goat is the Boynton crest and the stag a Strickland emblem. The intricate pattern involves flower, fruit and fleur-de-lis pendants suspended from eight-pointed stars. The internal half-octagonal porch reduced draughts and ensured privacy; its appearance is vaguely continental, explained by its early Renaissance design of 1568, stemming from northern Italy and Germany.

The Victoria & Albert Museum purchased the chamber in 1891 and returned it on permanent loan only as recently as 1999.

Sizergh Castle enjoys the shelter of Morecambe Bay and free-draining soil in a limestone area. The estate covers 6.48 square kilometres/1,600 acres, in the midst of which is a garden that includes two lakes. The highlight to the north of the castle is the rock garden, created between 1926 and 1928. The design was carried out by a local firm of landscapers (which still exists), T.R. Hayes and Sons of Ambleside, to a design by a local architect, Charles Henry Wearing. It was created for Lord Strickland's second wife, Margaret Hulton. It is the largest limestone rock garden belonging to the National Trust and includes part of the National Collection of hardy ferns, which flourish in its north-facing aspect. Specimen conifers add evergreen interest, while the changing seasons are registered by extensive plantings of Japanese maples, seductive in spring and spellbinding in autumn. Alpines and primulas add spring interest, and clumps of blue-flowered willow-leaved gentians add rhythm and repetition in late summer.

Sizergh Castle is easily accessible from the M6 and is close to Kendal, making it one of the most-visited houses in the county. It also enjoys national marketing and coverage by being owned by the National Trust. The castle has an events programme that presents the house in an imaginative way and highlights the furniture, gardens, historic landscape and natural history of the area. Architecture walks around the house and outbuildings are designed to pinpoint the key changes and alterations from the fourteenth century to the present. You can also learn about the estate – its ancient trees, birds, river, wildlife, orchard, honeybees and nearby Sizergh fell – through the changing seasons. Opening up rooms not always accessible has been a popular move, and the occasional opening of the Tudor kitchen with its historic pewter and copper is a big draw.

Remarkably, there is another fine Elizabethan house only a mile away at Levens Hall.

The rock garden, which features local limestone, with the garderobe and north-facing Elizabethan kitchen wing behind.

1170s	The original property of Henry II is granted to the Deincourt family.
1239	The start of the Strickland family's seven-century occupation of Sizergh, with the marriage of Elizabeth Deincourt to Sir William de Stirkeland. They prosper during the wars against the Scots and French, carrying the banner of St George at Agincourt.
1336	A grant from Edward III allows Sir Walter Strickland to enclose the land around Sizergh as his exclusive park. The fourteenth-century 18-metre/60-foot-high pele tower is built.
1400s	In the Wars of the Roses, the Stricklands side with the Yorkists, and under the Tudors make ambitious, prosperous marriages with the Parr and Neville families.
MID-1550s	The medieval house receives a major overhaul converting it into a fashionable Elizabthan house, with the hall raised to first-floor level, and the outbuildings which form the two Elizabethan wings.
1558–85	Sizergh receives interior makeovers with some of the finest oak-panelled interiors in the north of England.
1600s	Gambling debts bring poverty to the Strickland family but this lack of money preserves the castle from demolition or alterations.
EARLY 18TH-CENTURY	The Strickland family, Catholic supporters of the exiled James II, return to Sizergh from France. Although impoverished, the prudent Winifred Lady Strickland oversees baroque-style alterations.
1773–4	The wealthy Cecilia Strickland alters the first-floor hall to become a neo-classical saloon in the Georgian style, which is now the drawing room on the first floor.
1891	The inlaid chamber and its contents are sold to the Victoria & Albert Museum for £1,000, plus £400 for the bed.
1897–1902	The neo-gothic carriage entrance and new internal staircase were made.
1931	Lord Strickland transfers the estate to his daughter, Mary, and her husband, Henry Hornyold.
1950	With their son Lt-Cdr Thomas Hornyold-Strickland they give Sizergh to the National Trust. Sizergh opens to public for the first time.
1999	The entirety of the panelling is restored with a long-term loan.

LEVENS HALL

'Enfolding sunny spots of greenery'

Levens is remarkable for many things – not least its panelling, carved overmantels and ornate plasterwork – but especially for the fact that it is an Elizabethan gentleman's residence barely touched by time. The Grahme family, forebears of the present owners, the Bagots, owned several homes and they came to regard Levens Hall as a quiet home where family widows lived. As there was little pressure to follow fashion, upgrade the house or alter it dramatically, there were no great developments after 1686. Consequently, Levens Hall remains a fine example of an unspoilt Elizabethan house. The feeling that time has stood still here is echoed by the great volume of domestic papers that successive generations have retained. Levens Hall is still privately owned: it has been owned by the Bagot family since the eighteenth century and is currently in the hands of Hal and Susie Bagot.

The exterior of Levens represents three distinct periods. To understand the house it is best to view it from the north-facing front approach. The oldest surviving part is the medieval pele tower and hall (1250–1300) at its core but these have been hidden by various sixteenth-century extensions. You could be forgiven for thinking that the dominant square tower is the original pele tower, but it is in fact part of a new house of around 1580, built by James Bellingham, who inherited Levens in 1580. The major building work involved adding a separate dining room and servants' hall, drawing rooms and kitchens (the original kitchen would have been located externally to decrease the chance of fire spreading), creating the house you see today. After James Bellingham refurbished it in the 1580s, his great-grandson lost the whole estate by gambling, and legend has it that Levens was won with the turn of the ace of hearts. The next remarkable moment in its history was the sale to Colonel James Grahme in 1689, who added the south and west wings, including the brewhouse. A later tower of 1820 can be seen peeping out on the east elevation to the left.

Levens Hall has the world's oldest topiary garden, created in 1694.

ABOVE The north front. The
original pele tower is hidden
behind the dominant square
tower of 1580.
RIGHT ABOVE Elizabeth I's royal
coat of arms, the focal point of the
hall, is prominently displayed over
the fireplace, opposite the front
door, lest anyone should miss it,
making clear the family's loyalty to
Her Majesty.
RIGHT BELOW The ornate plaster
ceiling in the hall, with the
Bellingham bugle and deer.

The front door opens directly on to a light and spacious Elizabethan hall. This is made comfortable by a generous fireplace and an oak-panelled wainscot, and has an intricately plastered ceiling. As you enter, it is as if you are stepping back in time, for the hall has changed little since the reign of Elizabeth I; with its panelling and elaborate plasterwork it is a vivid reminder of that exuberant age.

Not only is the hall designed to impress: it confirms the Bellingham family's allegiance to the English Crown. Elizabeth's rival to the throne, Mary, Queen of Scots, and conspirators had been plotting to have Elizabeth murdered and place Mary on the throne in 1572; Mary was not executed until 1587. A sense of that uneasy period is immediately apparent with the coat of arms of Elizabeth I above the fireplace and the thirteen Bellingham shields displaying the family's bugle motif above the panelling. Shields also enliven the carved panelling, stained-glass windows and the ornate ceiling. The family's allegiance to the monarch is reinforced throughout the house.

Firearms and Civil War armour are also displayed over the fireplace. The Charles II candle sconces on the panelling are occasionally lit on special occasions.

One of the most memorable rooms is the dining room, in which the walls are covered in Cordova leather. Leather as an interior wall decoration was as familiar in the seventeenth century as wallpaper has become to us, but changing fashions ensured that most of the leather

FOLLOWING PAGES The Redman
Room, one of the bedrooms. A bust
of Charles I gazes down from the
top of a George II cabinet.

used to decorate walls has been removed. An inventory of 1697 indicates that this richly patterned Cordova leather is over three hundred years old. The pattern has a timeless appeal, and in the evening the colours glint and sparkle in a most beguiling fashion. The background design is busy with stylized flowers, leaves and stalks forcing their way upwards from the floor to the austere (for Levens) plaster ceiling, studded with the coats of arms of England, Scotland, France and Wales.

A set of Charles II hand-carved walnut dining chairs is said to be the finest in the land. The chairs are a rarity, because walnut is prone to woodworm and a great deal of walnut furniture has not survived. Look out for the initials of James Bellingham on the overmantel, dated 1586. The Bagot family continues to use this room for festivities.

The drawing room is a fine survivor of the Elizabethan period. The room used to be the great chamber and became Colonel Grahme's dining room from 1688. Its chief glory is a 1595 carved oak overmantel; the carving is regarded as being so stupendous that it appears in the American edition of the *Encyclopaedia Britannica*. Showing the family's allegiance to Elizabeth I, multiple coats of arms are framed in a two-tier arrangement of short columns, either singly or in pairs. The Elizabethans relished display. The walls and ceiling are steeped

Late seventeenth-century Cordova leather adorns the dining-room walls.

in period details: lozenge-patterned oak panelling, corner fluted pilasters and eight-pointed stars and quatrefoils on the white ribbed plaster ceiling that drip with pendants and chandeliers. Coats of arms in stained glass festoon the top of the bay window. En route to the small drawing room next door there is a carving of James Bellingham, holding his shield in a demure manner.

The small, or south, drawing room is more intimate and contains the enthralling carved chimneypiece of the Four Seasons and Five Senses. In the Elizabethan period, the use of the five senses was an indication of the pleasures of entertainment on offer at a great house, and would have been recognized as such at the time. Supported by an angry Samson and Hercules flanking the opening, the figures of Touch, Smell and Taste frame carved panels of the Four Elements and the Four Seasons above. The whole edifice is crowned with Hearing and Sight, reclining at ease in spite of being perched on the slanting broken pediment.

The Redman Room and the Bellingham Room are the two main bedrooms open to view. The carved oak panelling in the Redman Room is a good foil for the Portuguese four-poster bed, which was acquired in 1809. Furniture such as this would have made useful ballast for empty ships returning from depositing troops for the Peninsular Wars. Other furniture in the room, dating from the eighteenth century, did not have to travel so far, being supplied by Mr Gillow of Lancaster. The Bellingham Room is oak panelled with an elaborate ornate plaster ceiling seeming to defy gravity.

The dressing room contains a miracle of fine English patchwork: the earliest to have survived dating from 1708, with thirty-two stitches to the inch.

The garden at Levens is world famous, Grade I listed and Cumbria's leading historic garden, a superb example of formal topiary from the seventeenth century. The garden dates from 1688 and was inspired by the diarist and gardener John Evelyn, who encouraged Colonel James Grahme to pursue the then current trend for enhancing nature by opening vistas. Grahme had been impressed by the work of Monsieur Guillaume Beaumont, gardener to James II, so offered him a commission to design and construct the garden and park. Levens is his only surviving legacy. When Catherine, Countess of Suffolk and Berkshire, inherited Levens from her father, Colonel Grahme, in 1730, she retained the design because she felt that any changes would rob her of happy childhood memories.

Her widowed daughter-in-law, Mary, the Viscountess of Andover, decided to retire to Levens for the rest of her long life until 1803. The romantic allure of the garden appealed to her so much that she instructed her equally ancient gardener, Mr MacMillan, to do the minimum. Unfortunately he took her so literally that the next gardener, Mr Forbes, had to replace nearly 15 kilometres/ 9 miles of overgrown box hedging. By this time the viscountess's granddaughter, Mrs Greville Howard, had inherited Levens, as Colonel Grahme's last direct

CLOCKWISE FROM TOP LEFT The drawing room; the drawing-room fireplace of 1595, incorporating the coats of arms of Elizabeth I and the Bellingham family; a detail of a boy and a hound in the hall (above) and patterned plasterwork above the oak panelling in the hall (below); a modest James Bellingham above the door from the drawing room to the small drawing room.

descendant. When she died childless, her nephew by marriage, General Upton, inherited. He was followed by her father's great-great-nephew, Josceline Bagot, great-grandfather of Hal Bagot, the present owner.

Beaumont's quartered design compartmentalizes the flat garden with broad and towering beech hedges into smaller and intimate areas, which give rise to different gardens, each having their own identity and atmosphere. Chris Crowder, the head gardener since 1986, and only the tenth gardener in three hundred years, believes in using plants to create effects in order to establish the personality of an area. The topiary garden is the pièce de résistance, with remarkable sculpted yews set in box parterres.

The topiary figures inspire awe. Over a hundred shapes jostle for attention, some hunched like strange animals, some crooked and leaning, and some towering above the others, proudly asserting their perfect symmetry. These living sculptures even have their own individual names: the Bagot B, Judge's Wig, Great Umbrella, Howard Lion, Queen Elizabeth and her maids of honour, and the King and Queen chess pieces. In spite of their monumentality a lightness of touch abounds, with quirky giant birds, tottering cakestands and leaning corkscrews. It is tempting to imagine that these figures actually come to life after dark, like the toys in Respighi's ballet *La Boutique Fantasque*.

After decades of being unfashionable, by the early nineteenth century having a formal garden by the house coupled with 'a certain reverence for the past', as Chris Crowder describes it, had become more acceptable, and the topiary garden came to be recognized as a unique survivor of our gardening heritage. Old photographs and paintings reveal how cluttered the overstuffed Victorian design of herbaceous perennials, bulbs and roses looked amid the already satisfying structure of the topiary. Chris Crowder plants a single block of colour in each bed of the parterre, likening these carpets to 'steadying plinths beneath the detail and focus of the topiary sculptures above'. Thousands of black and white tulips crystallize the chessboard atmosphere. These are followed by antirrhinums, pale yellow marguerites, verbena and slabs of foliage bedding such as *Helichrysum petiolare* 'Limelight', all creating the impression that a giant has been busy embroidering on a grand scale. The bedding offers a complete change of seasonal planting and the schemes are never repeated.

The adjacent rose garden had become a spent force by the late 1980s, so repeat-flowering David Austin English roses, redolent of old roses, have been planted in fresh soil.

Elsewhere the garden enclosures within the beech hedges are larger and more informal. Bold planting demonstrates the value of simplicity in a complex design. The eastern boundary limestone wall has a long border running the length of it, in which shrubs with purple and gold foliage have been planted to give rhythm and repetition, and mask the wall. The coloured foliage has the additional advantage of contrasting with the green canopy of the trees growing outside and showing above the wall.

In this relaxing setting, there is further scope for contemplation within the great Beech Circle and among the ancient beech hedges. Such monumental trees, dividing the garden like living walls, do not seem to need any further plants. Incidentally, the hedges are best seen when the wild garlic (*Allium*

'White Triumphator' tulips in the box-edged borders of the topiary garden, with the park beyond.

ursinum) is in flower, its snowy white exuberance creating a memorable spring picture under the fresh beech foliage.

It will be apparent by now that in spite of its three hundred years' vintage the garden at Levens never stands still. Not only are there innovations in the planting: sometimes a whole area requires a new look. To mark the three hundredth anniversary in 1994 a new fountain garden was created. It has the primary benefit of blanking out some of the intrusive local traffic noise. The quartered design echoes Beaumont's and led to the creation of a circular pond and jet fountain within quadrant beds. These are delineated by pleached limes, which offer a contrast to the yew and beech elsewhere and provide the excitement of spring buds, giving way to the full leaf of summer before fabulous autumn tints emerge, followed by the winter tracery of branch, stem and twig.

Looking from the orchard to the *Ginkgo biloba* in the topiary garden.

As a grand finale, the contemplative peace of the Beech Circle is shattered by double fiery red borders, which prolong the season of interest by continuing to blaze away until well into late summer and early autumn. This area erupts with cannas and dahlias like a northern outpost of the late Christopher Lloyd's tropical plantings at Great Dixter in Sussex.

The park beyond the garden was a medieval deer park, formally restructured as a recreational deer park by Beaumont in 1700 with the great Oak Avenue, and ancient yew trees and specimen trees marking the change in fashion from formality to the love of nature in all its moods.

The world-famous topiary gardens provide Levens Hall with a unique selling point. Being family owned and a fine example of a largely unaltered Elizabethan house also make it attractive to visitors.

But the owners, Hal and Susie Bagot, are keenly aware that the relatively small scale of the house and formal gardens create limitations to the type of events they can host. They have found that the layout of the house and the size of the rooms do not lend themselves to large-scale gatherings. Although weddings have been welcomed in the past, the risk to the delicate fabric of the building began to overtake the pleasure of hosting them. The formal nature of the gardens, with its narrow turf paths (which soon wear away under pressure, especially after heavy rainfall) and the grass compartments within the beech hedging enclosures, severely reduces the number of open spaces available for large-scale outdoor events. This is not the place for rock concerts or even open-air theatre (always tricky in the Lake District, although held by some houses).

The challenge, therefore, has been to recognize what is feasible. So Hal and Susie Bagot have introduced one of the most unlikely events in cool Cumbria: the sizzling Lakes Chilli Fest in mid-August, which celebrates chilli-related

In the orchard tulips grow in squares of unmown grass under the trees.

items with talks and demonstrations. A major influence behind this is the success of the annual chilli event at West Dean in Sussex. Having checked that there was no conflict of interest, a date in mid-August was selected, and the weekend is going from strength to strength. Even so, the tramping of 6,000 chilli fans over two days makes its mark, literally, on turf that is well trodden anyway by late summer, so limited access to the more fragile areas has had to be introduced.

Meanwhile, pleasantly low-key activities such as annual visits from the Lakeland Car Club and the Bentley Owners' Club add lustre to the front of the house. Inside, occasional classical concerts for specially invited audiences bring the hall to life on winter evenings, and are an asset to the local community. The supportive band of season-ticket holders and regulars who make Levens a frequent lunch or coffee stop throughout the season are particularly valued.

The head gardener, Chris Crowder, also works as an ambassador for the gardens, presenting a 3-D illustrated talk to societies, or welcoming groups or individuals on home ground with gardener's walks on summer evenings. Every opportunity to breathe new life into the garden is seized. The fountain garden created for the tercentenary celebrations in 1994 achieved this, while the introduction of a new willow labyrinth in 2009 injected a new focus for children.

While acknowledging the public's hunger for novelty, Hal Bagot maintains that there are limits to the possibilities of reinventing a house built in 1580 which has retained its furnishings over the centuries. So it comes as something of a surprise that although the Bagots fight shy of hanging abstract modern art on their oak panelling, occasionally they have been radical with garden exhibitions. One of these was of Julia Barton's contemporary garden sculpture installations in 2000. Her bending and twisting of familiar garden materials such as steel poles, wire and rubber hose into eight sculptures echoing the existing topiary shapes, and then dressing them with alpine plants and succulents to show off their textures and colours, created several ripples in a garden famous for its time-honoured clipping of yew and box. The installations prompted visitors to consider the gardens in a new light.

One of the greatest challenges facing Hal and Susie Bagot in the running of Levens Hall is maintaining the structure of an ageing Elizabethan house. Thanks to decades of concentrated effort, the roof is in good shape and as with all old houses this is a cause for celebration. But the inevitable cost of ongoing maintenance is exacerbated by legislation that necessitates rejecting new materials and skills in favour of time-honoured practices: though kinder to the house and ensuring authenticity, these do not come cheap. Repairing chimneys with traditional lime mortar and hair is a case in point. Likewise leaded light windows tend to flex with the wind and wear out more quickly than less elaborate windows and replacing them involves expensive specialist work.

The threat of dry rot casts a huge shadow on any house of this vintage. If gutters and downspouts are left unchecked, they gradually fill with a formidable assortment of rotting leaves, silt and the inevitable 'small bits that keep dropping off'. If water is allowed to settle in a gutter because of such debris and then overflows during heavy rain, the damp that begins to seep into the walls can lead to the most awful damage. The target at Levens is to clean all the gutters and downspouts six times a year. Never an easy job, it is now more difficult, as ladders can no longer be used, owing to the raft of health and safety regulations in force. Having to use scaffolding or a cherry picker, operated where it can be manipulated easily, means that the whole job takes rather longer than is desirable. Inside, floorboards and lighting have to be monitored regularly to make sure they are in good order.

Fuel is an increasingly alarming and emotive subject for everyone living in Britain, including the Bagots. The nearest gas supply is a mile away from Levens Hall and an estimate of around £60,000 to bring a gas pipe here necessitates continuing reliance on oil heating. Spiralling costs for this are becoming crippling, so sustainable forms of heating that rely on woodchips and wood pellets are being investigated.

The successful operation of a house over four hundred years old requires special skills. Hal Bagot's parents felt he would be unable to continue as they had done, no matter how capable he might prove himself to be. Yet after thirty-five years' commitment, Hal Bagot, with his wife, Susie, has steered Levens Hall successfully into the twenty-first century. In the processs, he comments, he has learned about many things he never dreamed of as a young man (when he used to think he knew everything). The Bagots' eldest son, Richard, is now almost the same age as Hal Bagot was when he took over the reins from his father, and it will be Richard who determines the course that Levens takes in the future.

1170	William of Lancaster gives land to Norman de Hieland (Yealand), who becomes founder of the de Redman family.
c.1225–1578	De Redman family.
c.1580–1688	James Bellingham's family.
1562	Levens is sold to Sir Alan Bellingham.
1578	The last de Redman, Dorothy Layton, still alive, prevents Sir Alan from inheriting; he wills manor to son.
1580	His son James gains possession and creates much of Levens as seen today
SIXTEENTH CENTURY	Brewhouse built.
1603	James Bellingham welcomes James I as king, James knighted in Durham.
1641	Death of James Bellingham.
1689	Colonel James Grahme purchases Levens.
1690	Main doorway created.
1694–7	The topiary garden is laid out and planted by Guillaume Beaumont.
1701	Levens Park laid out also by Beaumont.
1709	Grahme's daughter Catherine marries Henry Bowes Howard, 4th Earl of Berkshire, and provides Grahme with grandchildren.
1730	Grahme dies and estate passes to Catherine.
1745	Her husband 4th Earl of Berkshire inherits earldom of Suffolk; Levens is only one of his several houses and estates, rather than the main family seat, hence little incentive to change the garden.
1757	Lord Suffolk dies and Catherine refuses to rent to a tenant who wishes to sweep away the gardens and park in favour of sheep and cattle grazing, or any other tenant for that matter.
1762	Catherine dies; estate passes to grandson Henry Howard. Levens becomes the home of his widowed mother, Mary Howard, Lady Andover, for over forty years.
1803	Mary Howard dies and estate passes to her daughter Frances Howard. Frances had married Richard Bagot, who had taken her surname.
1807	Daughter Mary Howard, last of Grahme's direct descendants, marries Colonel Upton, who takes the Howard name too.
1817	Frances dies and Mary inherits.
1820	Four-storey Howard Tower for Mary Howard completed. Mary and husband visit Levens on alternate autumns, dividing their time among several homes.
1846	Colonel Howard dies, Mary lives for over thirty more years.
1877	Mary Howard dies and her husband's nephew, General the Hon. Arthur Upton, inherits having spent some of his time here since 1866.
1883	Arthur dies without issue. Josceline Bagot, Mary Howard's father's great-great nephew, inherits.
1896	Birth of son, Alan Desmond Bagot, first direct male heir for 200 years
1913	Josceline Bagot dies, Alan inherits.
1920	Alan dies of pneumonia; Levens reverts to his uncle Richard Bagot, who dies 1921.
1921	Seven-year-old Oliver Robin Gaskell inherits, Josceline's nephew through his daughter Dorothy Gaskell. Levens let to Reynolds family, Lancashire cotton mill owners.
1936	Oliver assumes name of Bagot by Royal Licence and marries in 1938.
SECOND WORLD WAR	Oliver captured and in German prisoner-of-war camps for much of the war. His wife, Annette, manages to change potentially damaging billet of soldiers on Levens so house allocated to nuns instead.
1960s	Ministry of Transport threatens to run dual carriageway M6 link through the end of Levens Park. Oliver Bagot employs two QCs and wins case against it.
1975	Oliver and Annette retire from running Levens and Hal and Susie Bagot take over.

SWARTHMOOR HALL

'With holy dread'

Together with Townend near Windermere (see page 56), Swarthmoor Hall, near Ulverston, is a remarkable example of domestic architecture dating back to the sixteenth century. The survivor of a larger building, this late Elizabethan manor is regarded as the cradle of Quakerism and deserves to be better known.

The original house of 1586 was owned by George Fell, a major landowner in the Furness district. It was then inherited by his son, Judge Thomas Fell, and his wife, Margaret. As well as observing the compulsory attendance at the local parish church, Judge Fell and Margaret would often have prayers at home, attend 'lecture days' and listen to travelling preachers. One of these was George Fox, who noted their tradition of hospitality and way of life in June 1652. Fox believed that the trappings of established religion (buildings, symbols and the priesthood) were unnecessary and could be corrupting. He also held notions of

Swarthmoor Hall's roughcast walls and stone mullioned windows are typical of Lakeland vernacular architecture.

equality that were thought dangerous, and had been subjected to persecution and imprisonment, but by the time he discovered the Fells, he already had an enthusiastic following.

While her husband was away, Margaret Fell found Fox's ideas most persuasive and on one occasion when Judge Fell was returning across Morecambe Bay an advance party alerted him to the news that his household was bewitched. Fortunately Judge Fell could see more clearly than most people in those intolerant times and, respecting his wife, listened to what Fox had to say. Without joining Fox, he continued to attend Ulverston Church, yet allowed his home to be used as a meeting place for the Quakers, so called because they would quake or tremble in awe of God. Having thus distanced himself, he had placed himself in a better position to support and defend the Quakers, formally known as the Religious Society of Friends. In this way Swarthmoor Hall was the birthplace of the Quaker movement – which expanded significantly in the following years – and became its first headquarters and northern home. In time the movement permeated the British Isles, the Americas and continental Europe.

Judge Fell died in 1658 and Margaret married George Fox eleven years later in 1669. They promoted the movement together, travelling widely and blazing with missionary zeal in spite of constant persecution and the threat of imprisonment, until Fox himself died in 1691. Margaret survived him by twelve years until her death in 1702, in her eighty-eighth year, and the Fells' youngest daughter Rachel, who had married Daniel Abraham, inherited the hall.

After the hall was sold in 1759 it fell into disrepair during the occupancy of a succession of tenant farmers over the following 150 years. By the late eighteenth century a substantial part had been pulled down. During this time, although not in Quaker ownership, it remained a place of pilgrimage.

Salvation came at last in 1912 when Emma Clarke Abraham (a direct descendant of Daniel and Rachel Abraham) bought the hall and began to restore it sympathetically. She unblocked sealed-up windows, reinstated the balcony, constructed an entrance arch bearing her initials and extended the south-west wing. The front of the house was originally the side facing the town of Ulverston, and the present entrance, more convenient for the stable block, used to be the back door. Emma Clarke Abraham left the rare example of a smaller Elizabethan manor that we see today, and it has been carefully maintained by the Society of Friends since 1954, when it purchased the house from her nephew. The house gradually came to be furnished in the style of the late seventeenth century and the most recent renovations took place in 2000. It continues to operate today as a Quaker meeting house.

Emma Clarke Abraham re-established the idea of an Elizabethan hall. The great hall is thought to have been the communal dining room for the family; whether or not the early Quakers held their meetings here is uncertain. Although none of the furniture is original to this room, the pieces represented are in keeping with the period. The carved press or court cupboard by the bay window was a general-purpose store cupboard.

The great hall, refurbished by Emma Clarke Abraham after 1912.

ABOVE Thomas Fell's study, where he would eavesdrop on religious meetings taking place in the adjacent great hall.
RIGHT ABOVE A 1670s travelling bed in George Fox's bedroom.
RIGHT BELOW Margaret and Thomas Fell's bedroom. The lower area of the ornate carved headboard would have been covered by bolsters and was therefore left plain.

Judge Thomas Fell's study at Swarthmoor Hall became a retreat. Without taking part, Fell would sit here when there were meetings in the adjacent great hall and hear what was being said. As in much of the house, the panelling and carving are not original and are again the work of Emma Clarke Abraham after 1912. The 'Great Bible' from 1541 is one of the oldest artefacts, although not original to the house; it would have resided in a church, secured by its chain. The travelling writing desk ensured that work could still go on away from home, and be transported on horseback.

Bedrooms and beds are particularly well represented in this house. The rooms comprise Margaret and Thomas Fell's bedroom, Margaret Fell's bedroom, Gerorge Fox's bedroom and an attic room. Some of these rooms are panelled or painted white, and have crisp white beamed ceilings. Colourful rugs are scattered on the old oak floors and the furnishings indicate a simple existence.

Margaret and Thomas's bedroom has also been known as the 'parlour' or 'Fell's Office'. The panelling is now recognized as being early eighteenth century, and one school of thought considers that the fifteenth- and sixteenth-century carvings to be by the same Continental craftsmen who worked on the choir stalls in Cartmel Priory. Their bed is the one original piece of furniture in the house. All nine of Fell children may have been born in it. Originally a full-tester, the tester has long disappeared and the footposts were removed by Emma Clarke Abraham when she had one split to form a frame for the study fireplace. The cradle (which

would have remained with the nurse rather than the parents) has two hatches. The lower one is thought to have been used either as a warming pan or for the easy removal of soiled bedding. Vivid reminders of a vanished world abound, such as the rush light holders and the candle box – made of metal rather than timber to prevent rats scavenging for the wax – sitting on the window ledge. The saltbox was placed next to the fireplace to prevent damp from spoiling an expensive and vital commodity.

Margaret Fell's bedroom was the room which she used in the last years of her long life. A full-tester bed in all its glory is the highlight; it is over 1.75 metres/6 feet long and narrower than a modern standard double. Behind the bed there is a reminder of the house's mixed fortunes, as the panelling is clearly from another dwelling. As in Margaret and Thomas Fell's bed, the rich carving on the headboard ends abruptly at bolster level. This was because people would often sleep propped up on a bolster (a long underpillow), and the continuation of carving below the bolster line was regarded as an unnecessary expense.

Dominating George Fox's room is a travelling bed dating from the 1670s and made of lignum vitae, the heaviest timber in the world; the bed needs two horses to drag its estimated 1 ton weight. It was a gift from the Quaker plantation owners in Barbados which Fell received while he was travelling along America's east coast. The mechanism for tightening the rope base is still intact.

The attic bedroom is so light and spacious that it is not clear whether this was used as servants' quarters or as a workroom for the storage and spinning of flax.

The full-tester bed in the attic room once belonged to Fox's friend Robert Widders of Yealand Redmayne, near Carnforth in Lancashire.

The gardens at Swarthmoor Hall include formal gardens to the front and east side of the house, an orchard and fruit area, meadow and woodland. Much emphasis is placed on sustainability. Bees are encouraged with nectar plants such as lavender, which is also a natural moth deterrent

LEFT A studded chest, with George Fox's initials and the date 1675. It is thought to be one he brought out of Worcester jail.
OPPOSITE A stone mullioned window in the great hall.

1586	The house is built, and in due course owned by Judge Thomas Fell, Chancellor of the Duchy of Lancaster, and his wife, Margaret.
1652	George Fox, one of Quakerism's founding fathers, visits.
1658	Death of Thomas Fell.
1660	Fox is arrested at Swarthmoor for his beliefs.
1661	Nationwide persecution of Quakers.
1664	Margaret is imprisoned for her beliefs for four years in Lancaster, having become leader of the Quaker movement in the north.
1668	Margaret is released.
1669	Margaret marries Fox in Bristol.
1670–71	Margaret's second Lancaster imprisonment and release. Fox leaves for America until June 1673.
1676	Swarthmoor is valued at £450.
1678	Fox's last visit to Swarthmoor; he stays until March 1680.
1691	Death of George Fox.
1702	Death of Margaret Fox in her eighty-eighth year, at Swarthmoor.
1759	The grandson of Thomas and Margaret, John Abraham, having fallen into debt, sells the hall to Captain Lindow of Lancaster. It remains in his family until 1912.
1912	Fell's descendant Emma Clarke Abraham buys and restores the house.
1954	The house and 53 hectares/130 acres are sold to the Society of Friends.
2000	Extensive renovations and improvements to the facilities.

and is dried to protect the hall's textiles. A local beekeeper keeps several hives in the grounds and the bees help to pollinate the orchard trees and fruit bushes.

The meadow begins with purple crocus in February, followed by narcissi and then grasses and herb species for a summer hay crop. A wild meadow with herbs and several varieties of grasses has been established through not using fertilizers (natural or man-made). Along the edge of this meadow is a recent plantation of oaks that will be ready for harvesting in two hundred years' time if required. Wild roses, nettles and thistles are all left to flourish and to encourage wildlife; decomposing woodpiles attract birds, small mammals, insects and fungi. The ivy is allowed to grow on the walls to provide low-quality nectar in autumn and provide a good home for insects and small mammals, but it is cut back hard every year to prevent it from pulling the wall over.

The orchard, fruit trees and bushes plus mature beech trees and woodland make this garden something of a little paradise. A workshop area includes compost bins and logs seasoning for use in the hall.

As the cradle of Quakerism, Swarthmoor Hall places an emphasis on spiritual reflection and runs several events relevant to the Religious Society of Friends. The addition of a new conference room for up to fifty has made the hall accessible to a new market. Hands-on activities as diverse as textile making and a practical workshop on drystone walling take place here. Day trips from Swarthmoor highlight local places of interest relating to George Fox's life. The hall also prides itself on the variety of volunteering activities it offers. Conservation, gardening, history and office support make up the various options, so that you can do anything from indexing the archives or researching historical information to helping with general maintenance or recording wildlife. There is also a thriving Friends of Swarthmoor Hall scheme. The hall stays open throughout the year, and welcomes schools and group visits.

TOWNEND

'Of fertile ground'

Townend helps us to understand the layout and evolution of the Cumbrian farmhouse and vernacular architecture. Located in the village of Troutbeck, near Windermere, it dates back to the late sixteenth or early seventeenth centuries, and has been developed and added to over the centuries. It is also significant for being owned by one family, the Brownes, for over four hundred years. It has been owned by the National Trust since 1948.

The prominent Westmorland round chimneys are a key vernacular feature. Looking at the south front you can see how Townend developed into a substantial dwelling. The central section between the chimneys was the original firehouse. This would have been the most important room, possibly part of a long-gone larger structure or standing on its own as a room used for meals and entertaining. To the right on the east side you can see the down house or kitchen, with a central entrance passage called the hallan, or hallway, running between the two rooms and replacing the firehouse's original front door. The down house was built a few steps lower than the firehouse as it was used by animals, so that the waste would run away from the 'high end'.

To the rear of the firehouse, the north wing is likely to have been built in the late seventeenth century to create a more imposing staircase, a parlour, which has since become the library, and a 'great room' on the first floor, which we would recognize as the master bedroom and which is known at Townend as the state bedroom. It is thought that the west wing may date back to 1739, when the accounts mention a 'New House' being built. This coincided with the need for more accommodation for a growing family at the time.

The dairy in the south-eastern corner is likely to date from the nineteenth century, perhaps modelled on a former buttery. Visitors today enter via the front door directly into the kitchen.

Townend demonstrates vernacular Lake District architecture with its limewashed render, Westmorland cylindrical chimneys and slate roof with oak mullioned windows.

OPPOSITE In the kitchen the haphazard arrangement of cupboards and a long-case clock incorporates eighteenth-century furniture and nineteenth-century carved pieces by the last George Browne.
LEFT Slate steps lead up from the kitchen to the housekeeper's bedroom.

The firehouse was the location for family meals and entertaining. Also known as the houseplace or simply house, the firehouse was the main heated ground-floor room in the centre of a Lakeland farmhouse; it was the hub where visitors would be entertained. The focal point of the room is appropriately the fireplace, now a gothic chimneypiece, which replaced a large stone chimneyhood in 1842–3. The old hood, under which people could sit close to the fire, wearing a hat to protect them from soot falling on wet days, called hallan-drop, was superseded when the cast-iron grate was introduced.

The beauty of the carved oak in this room is one of the highlights of Townend. The room boasts a seventeenth-century table so immense that it must surely have been brought into the house in pieces and assembled *in situ*. This table or 'board' would have been the hub of the house in the 1730s, where the family and 'boarders', servants and farmhands would have congregated for meals. An ornately carved oak press or a bread cupboard is a familiar sight in northern farmhouses and Townend has a fine example to the left of the fireplace, probably dating from the 1670s. Clap bread, a thin oat bread that helped to sustain Cumbrian folk into the 1890s, would have been stored in it.

The kitchen or down house is thought to have been added to the firehouse between 1623 and 1626. It contains one of the more intriguing aspects of Townend: a bewildering array of oak cupboards, drawers and shelves. The haphazard effect derived from their random placing is enchanting, and the long-case clock seeming to emerge from the low cupboard beneath it is almost comic. The heavily geometric patterns on the door and drawer fronts are the

LEFT Wallpaper recreated from a fragment designed by William Morris discovered in the library.
RIGHT ABOVE Library shelves made and carved by the last George Browne.
RIGHT BELOW More examples of George Browne's wood carving.

work of the last George Browne (1834–1914), and like the cast-iron range, which is nineteenth century, not quite as old as one would think on first sight. A meat loft within the chimney and accessed from the first floor was used for drying meat.

The library, formerly the parlour, is one of the three best libraries owned by the National Trust. A library in a country house is a familiar sight, but a yeoman farmer's library in a farmhouse is something of a rarity. You expect to find the Bible and reference books on religion, law, medicine and farming, and all these are represented. This library, though, is unique: it is famous not only for its serious works but also for those mass-produced stories and ballads printed as chap-books for ordinary folk. These booklets were once so commonplace that they were not regarded as collector's items, and consequently only a handful remain: those preserved at Townend are the only examples. A title such as *The Crafty Chamber-Maid's Garland* – a hilarious romp in which the heroine marries the rich farmer's son – gives a flavour of the material's calibre.

Father and son, 'Old Ben' and 'Young Ben' (1692–1748) – the only Bens among the many Georges who were owners – laid down the foundations of the library in the first half of the eighteenth century. They became a formidable book-buying duo. Father was busy collecting books on his doorstep at various Troutbeck auctions. Meanwhile his son, working as a writing master in a lawyer's office in London, sent him books from the capital. We know this from the extravagant signatures in his books; it must have been irresistible to practise his flowing hand. By 1740 there were around four hundred books in the library. The titles are written in ink on the page edges, because books used to be stored in chests before they were displayed on shelves.

The last George Browne's love of wood carving was a major influence on this room. His handiwork includes the bookshelves, chimneypiece, rush-bottomed chairs and other pieces. The Victorian William Morris wallpaper is a replica of a fragment discovered in the room and created in 1992. The Herdwick wool-mix carpet was woven locally by one Mr William Birkett in 1768 and is a reversible double cloth called a Scotch or Kidderminster.

MID-15THC	First mention of the Browne family in Troutbeck.
1525	First record of George Browne, yeoman, living at Townend.
LATE 16TH/EARLY 17THC	The firehouse – a single main room – is built.
1623–6	The down house or kitchen is added after the marriage of George Browne (1596–1685) and Susannah Rawlinson.
1667	George Browne (1626–1703) becomes High Constable of Kendal Ward.
LATE 17THC	The north wing is built, incorporating a former parlour, now the library, and the state bedroom above.
1739	The 'New House' or west wing (not open) is built.
19THC	The dairy is built at the south-east corner of kitchen. The last George Browne (1834–1914) adds new fireplaces and interior fittings.
1914	Cousin Richard (1876–1944) inherits and sells to Oswald Hedley.
1945	Death of Hedley. The Treasury accepts Townend in satisfaction of Estate duty.
1947	Townend is transferred to the National Trust, which purchases the seventeenth-century barn opposite and 324 hectares/801 acres.
1948	Opened to the public.

ABOVE LEFT Influenced perhaps by similar work at Sizergh and Levens, George Browne carved these family coats of arms, supported by mermen.
ABOVE RIGHT The state bed, or guest bed, dated 1672, bears the initials of George and Ellinor Browne.
BELOW The main bedroom with an anonymous 1842 portrait of the last George Browne, at the age of eight, reflected in the mirror.

Although it is unlikely that royalty was ever expected, in the master bedroom, or state bedroom, on the first floor of the north wing there is a 'state bed' with the initials of George and Ellinor, dated 1672, which would have been reserved for guests. This may give a clue to the building date of this extension. The bed hangings, hand woven locally in 1985, are based on a pattern copied from an old photograph. Something of a bedroom suite emerges, with a cradle dated 1670 and a linen chest of 1692.

In Victorian times it was common for older pieces of furniture, particularly oak, to be carved. The unmistakable hand of George Browne is easy to spot on the fire surround, redolent of the great Elizabethan wood carving at Levens and Sizergh. The raw-boned, broad-chested figures dwindling into fishtails and supporting coats of arms are delightfully naive. George also seems to have been busy working on the washstand and table mirror.

The cottage garden at Townend is a refreshing antidote to the larger and splendid country house gardens in the county. As well as his legacy as wood-carver in the house, the last George Browne had a great influence on the garden, both in his choice of plants and in its design. A keen gardener with a passion for colour, he favoured cottage-garden perennials, herbs, vegetables and fruit and this style of gardening has been continued by the National Trust. His copious notes have guaranteed that the partial re-creation of the garden is very much in the spirit of how he knew it.

Much of the garden is to the front of the house and enjoys a south-facing aspect. Endearingly, George's notes include many of the problems – such as rosebay willow herb and snails – that beset gardeners today. Plants close to George's heart included perennial phlox (he planted twenty-eight varieties in 1909 in alphabetical order), sweet peas, delphiniums and pansies. Appropriately in a cottage garden, George also cultivated herbs and vegetables and created an orchard with apples, plums, greengages and damsons. Records show that the Browne family's planting of the yew trees in 1736 was by a Tommy Benson and his son for all of two shillings.

The National Trust's policy at Townend, mainly because of the limited parking and the narrow lanes in the vicinity, is to hold a handful of low-key events during the year. These include unique items in the programme such as a focus on the library which have proved very popular. Visitors can also learn about behind-the-scenes work such as book conservation and how the house is put to bed at the end of the season. Seasonal activities range from an Easter egg hunt to a Hallowe'en trail in the garden. A meet-the-gardener tour is a popular attraction in National Trust gardens; on the tour of Townend's garden, visitors are surprised to learn that the gardener here attends on a weekly rather than a daily basis.

DALEMAIN

'Through wood and dale'

Dalemain is a predominantly Georgian mansion, enjoying a parkland setting close to the northern reaches of Ullswater with views of the Lakeland fells. Sir Edward Hasell bought Dalemain in 1679 and his descendants have owned it ever since. The present owners are Robert and Jane Hasell-McCosh.

The original Norman pele tower dates back to the twelfth century. Following the addition of a medieval hall, Dalemain was converted into a manor house with two forward-projecting wings in Elizabethan times. Rather like tradesmen, visitors today arrive in the rear courtyard to find the medieval hall and Elizabethan roughcast-stone manor house with its wings of three-storey barns. Apart from a discreet plant sales area and the occasional sign, the courtyard still looks much as it must have done for centuries.

If you stand on the front doorstep of Dalemain, you have placed yourself on the threshold of a Georgian mansion. The elegant façade, comprising the east front and the south elevation, dates from the mid-eighteenth century and was undoubtedly intended to impress visitors. Built in 1744, this elevation was the inspiration and possibly the design of Edward Hasell – the son of Sir Edward Hasell – and he evidently used the finest materials. Nine bays of pinky-grey ashlar (dressed stone), quarried locally at Stainton, with the central five bays separated by even quoins, stare out proudly across the parkland. The ashlar is very impacted and so strong that it has belied the weathering of 250 years.

Family and historic portraits, crowned with mounted red deer stag heads from the estate, lend Dalemain's entrance hall much of its atmosphere; apparently, it is something of a mystery how the occasional mothball leaps from the stag heads' ears on to the stairs. When all the doors are open, the hall affords a fine view of the enfilade of rooms running the length of the east front.

The wide and generous oak treads of the cantilever staircase, made from pit-sawn estate oak, weave their way upwards with a continuous moulded tassel-motif handrail. The joinery throughout the house is of a high standard and one

The 1744 Georgian 'new house' obliterates the pele tower and Elizabethan wings from view.

of the joys of Dalemain. It is said that the presence of an amnesty button on the turn of the handrail, inserted by the joiner, was an indication to other craftsmen that the family were good employers. Perhaps it was also an indication of how much they had enjoyed working at Dalemain.

Certainly Edward and Julia Hasell had a conciliatory approach to others. In the days of Bonnie Prince Charlie, they left instructions that if the rebel Highland army stationed in Penrith during the November of 1745 marched on the house, they were to be offered provisions and hay. Consequently the house escaped being ransacked.

The impressive canvas of the Piazzetta di San Marco looking towards San Giorgio Maggiore by Michele Marieschi was discovered rolled up in the attic by Robert Hasell-McCosh's parents. An unashamedly nostalgic and evocative 1920s portrait by Edmond Brock of Robert's father, Bryce McCosh, as a boy, dressed for a summer beach holiday, is one of the highlights on the staircase.

The old medieval hall is now the tea room, where the fireplace with its Jacobean chimneypiece makes a focal point, especially when a fire is lit on chilly days. The original barn-like roof beams have been obscured by a low ceiling that was inserted in 1550.

The dining room is still used by the family on special occasions. Portraits of bygone Hasells share the walls with more recent owners: Robert Hasell-McCosh's parents, Mrs Sylvia McCosh and her husband, Bryce McCosh. The Amritsar rug was specially made for this room, commissioned by Dorothea Hasell in the 1850s, when her husband's younger brother served in India with the Bengal Native Infantry. Like the Marieschi canvas, it had been stored in the attic, had been forgotten and was discovered along with some pelmets that have also been returned to the room, with new drapes. Again the joinery is of immaculate quality: the floorboards are particularly close fitting and the long tapering joins between them demonstrate first-rate craftsmanship.

A smaller dining room, the exquisite Chinese Room, is the most charming room in the house. The hand-painted paper dates from 1757 and still has the power to astonish. An exotic forest is brought vividly to life with a delicate tracery of twigs teeming with Asian pheasants, birds, brilliant butterflies and frighteningly overscaled insects. This curious menagerie would have been added once the paper had been hung to balance the design. The paper was last cleaned in the 1920s. The exotic theme is continued with snapping dragons on the rococo 'Chinese Chippendale' chimneypiece. Robert and Jane Hasell-McCosh are keen to maintain the impression that Dalemain remains a living family home and the full-length portrait of Jane supports this.

The drawing room gleams with polished oak, crystal chandelier and ornate mirrors. The warm woodwork and family portraits make it a cosy and welcoming room. Oak from the estate's forest of Barton provided the panelling. Pride of place is given to a Lely portrait of a most important individual in Dalemain's

ABOVE LEFT The staircase and entrance hall.
ABOVE RIGHT The Chinese Room, with its hand-painted wallpaper of 1757.
BELOW LEFT 'Mrs Mouse's house on the back stairs'.
BELOW RIGHT The dining room.

CURARUM DULCE LEVAMEN

The Oak Room, with a corner closet to the left.

history: Sir Edward Hasell. He bought Dalemain in 1679 from the trustees of Sir William Layton, whose family had owned the house since the thirteenth century. A pair of ornate mirrors from the Adam workshop flanking it adds a touch of the fanciful amid the order and sobriety.

The Oak Room or bedroom is a reminder that the house had Elizabethan roots before the Georgian addition of 1744 altered the front elevation. The richly polished panelling is sixteenth century; the painted panelling and most of the furniture are Georgian. The closet in the corner was originally the location of a staircase from the hall below, and when this eventually disappeared over centuries of reconstruction the remaining recess lent itself to becoming a small or side private chapel. The reeded mahogany single four-poster is of Hepplewhite design.

The Print Room reminds us of the days before photography and postcards and is named after a collection of early eighteenth-century prints with scenes portraying England and abroad.

Dalemain has had many keen gardening owners since the Hasell family arrived in 1679. The more recent history of the garden to the present day owes much to the labour and love of four remarkable women.

When Sir Edward Hasell bought Dalemain the garden had a typical emphasis on culinary and medicinal plants rather than flowers, but less than a decade later he began to revolutionize it by introducing the long terrace wall and a wide grass walk with the sundial as a focal point. A hundred years later, during the baroque period, the garden had the features of the time,

The garden, seen here from
the terrace, with the borrowed
landscape of the fells beyond.

with yew walks and topiary much in evidence. As the eighteenth century progressed, so did the landscaping of the parkland. The impression of a continuous view from the house came about when the river banks were walled. A weir, where the Dacre Beck flows into the river Eamont, was constructed to create a lake to be seen from the house.

Dorothea Hasell, who came to Dalemain in 1826, introduced some of the foundations we can still see and enjoy today, such as the formal nineteenth-century garden and the long south-facing herbaceous border on the terrace. One of the landmarks in the garden, an *Abies cephalonica* at the end of the terrace walk, is thought to have been presented by Joseph Banks, who sailed with Dorothy's uncle, James King, on HMS *Endeavour* under Captain Cook. It is the largest in the UK.

Huge changes in society and the aftermath of the First World War severely affected the efforts of Gertrude Hasell, who came from London to a cold, draughty, old-fashioned Dalemain in 1920. Lack of available manpower led her to follow the ideas of William Robinson, who promoted gardens without boundaries, merging seamlessly into the landscape of woodland and meadow beyond. Her struggle during the economic decline of the 1930s culminated in her seeing much of the garden ploughed up for the war effort.

After the Second World War the future of many country houses, regarded as anachronisms, was perhaps more grim than it had been since 1918. Dalemain survived, however, and the garden found salvation in Robert Hasell-McCosh's mother, Sylvia. She had been passionate about

propagation since childhood and had already become a talented and knowledgeable gardener when she took over the running of the house. Inspired by her garden in Lanarkshire and with a plantswoman's eye, she gradually began to replant the dormant garden during the 1960s and 1970s. Perhaps her greatest legacy is an astonishing sea of Himalayan blue poppies (*Meconopsis grandis*), which flourish in cool northern gardens. She was also responsible for extensive shrub plantings and over a hundred old-fashioned roses. This was a golden age for the garden.

After Sylvia McCosh's death in 1991, her daughter-in-law, Jane Hasell-McCosh, had a tough act to follow but she was determined to build on the good work to make the garden even more of an outstanding plantsman's garden. The aim to replace familiar plants with more interesting ones of the same variety continues to this day. Fortunately Jane had been a keen kitchen gardener as a child and found her feet at Dalemain quickly. She has wanted to promote the garden as understandable and accessible. Inspired by her own children from the days when she would entertain them with stories as they made their way through the garden, she has created a special children's garden, containing plants with animals in their names. She continues to takes an active interest, sharing ideas and feelings with her team, and building on the idea of the garden's strength being that it is foremost a personal place, rather than being known for, say, any great architectural structure or grandiose planting.

Today the garden at Dalemain is manned by part-time staff of a head gardener and a small team, some of whom attend for only one day per week. They all possess an individual skill, whether it be as a groundsman, in propagation or in preparing plants for gardening sales. Five volunteers bring further individual experience and enthusiasm; they are responsible for their own areas, so that they can take a real pride in gardening here. From this we can safely say that the garden is not overstaffed, but although at certain times of year Jane feels that William Robinson's ideas on gardens merging into the natural landscape are being taken to the limit, she recognizes that visitors are drawn to the atmosphere as well as the plantings, which over-manicuring would kill stone dead. Visitors also like the way the garden is divided into relatively small areas with which they can identify. A nice touch, especially in one of England's damper counties, is the invitation to make a complimentary repeat visit if the weather has been particularly inclement.

Jane classifies Dalemain as a north country family mansion with few airs and graces, and the family likes to feel that its home relates to the community. Over 2,000 Cumbrian folk were

involved in the building and their descendants continue to have a soft spot for this appealing and special place.

Dalemain's unique selling point is that it is a fine example of Georgian country house architecture within the county. Like many of the houses of the Lake District, it is not a treasure house. Nevertheless, part of its attraction is that the experience is of a high quality, and its location away from the central Lakes means that the number of visitors seldom exceeds the optimum. Visitors have the choice of a guided tour the moment the house opens, or are free to wander by themselves soon afterwards. Outside, where there is more space, there is scope to increase the number of garden visitors and to maximize the seasonal variation and interest.

The Hasell-McCosh family have energized their programme of events in recent years to help the season roll along. They start the season early with the World's Original Marmalade Competition in February, the Grand Prix of marmalade, complete with its own workshop. Jane is not only passionate about marmalade but regards it as an enjoyable team activity, fondly recalling making marmalade with her mother. Having grown concerned that marmalade was no longer attended to at breakfast in the way it once was, she discovered Elizabeth Rainbow's seventeenth-century recipes in Dalemain's archive and realized the huge potential of taking marmalade seriously. The World's Original Marmalade Festival was born in 2005 and has since flourished to become an international event; one Christmas Eve Jane had a Portuguese gentleman telephoning to enquire why his marmalade was not setting. The normal breathing space after Christmas has now vanished as entries from home and abroad start flooding in for the mid-February festival. Entry fees are dedicated to the Hospice at Home charity.

Dalemain's second biggest event is the Garden Festival in late June, which Jane likes to think of as a gentle affair that focuses on all aspects of gardens and gardening. Excellent links have been forged with the local college at Newton Rigg, which in turn has led to innovations in the garden. A defensive bank to prevent the river from flooding lent itself to the students creating a sleeping giant. Even the dark autumn days are lightened with apple celebrations in the tea room. Dalemain has many Victorian varieties of apple flourishing in the walled garden, and Jane would like to enlarge the collection, having studied the archives and found many different Georgian apples that they could also be cultivating. Seasonal fare in the tea room is very much a part of Dalemain's philosophy, so autumn sees a proliferation of recipes that include apples.

LEFT AND RIGHT Dalemain's
marmalade competition, held
every February, has become an
international event.

Other events are very much what you come to expect and enjoy about country houses in the summer, including north-west carriage driving in May, a food and craft fair, a vintage tractor club and shows of subjects as diverse as classic cars and fell pony stallions. The great winter shutdown is fast becoming a thing of the past. The tea room in the medieval hall is very much at the heart of Dalemain and has become almost a twelve-month operation. It now stays open until mid-December with Christmas lunches and opens again in early February, offering a blazing fire to those first intrepid visitors of the season who have come to enjoy the snowdrop and aconite walk. A flourishing Friends' group enjoys complimentary tickets to the house and gardens.

Robert and Jane Hasell-McCosh make the point that living in and running a large house and estate is very much a younger person's way of life. Dalemain is a mansion and often cold. Paradoxically, sizeable though it is, it is short of utility spaces where everyday practical jobs can to be carried out. This is not just a present-day problem: in the Victorian age knife polishing had to be undertaken in passages and even small dressing areas were carved out of landings. Fortunately Jane enjoyed the support of her mother-in-law, Sylvia, who shed light on how to adapt to living and working in Dalemain before she died in 1991.

Jane acknowledges that the house and garden are wonderful places in which to bring up her three children, Hermione, Beatrice and George, and she hopes that she and Robert have instilled in them their own values of seeing Dalemain as a family home which they love and care about, rather than a source of revenue. They both believe that it is the family that makes a house special and to them Dalemain is a family house with an absorbing history. They hope that when their son George takes over he will be able to cope.

12THC	The pele tower is built. First recorded mention in reign of Henry II (1154–89), one of a line of border towers to protect the country from the Scots.
14THC	The medieval hall is added.
16THC	Two further wings housing kitchen and living quarters create the Elizabethan manor house.
1679	Sir Edward Hasell buys the house.
1680s	A new hall, large window openings, new front door, new terrace and terrace wall (sundial) are added.
1686	In the garden the terraced walks and ha-has are made.
1744	The Georgian front of pink sandstone is built on the south-east and south-west sides.
1750	The south-west elevation is reconstructed and work continues on incorporating the old house into a new front parapet all the way round. This is the last of the major additions.
1960s–70s	The Rose Walk is created.

CONISHEAD PRIORY

'Holy and enchanted'

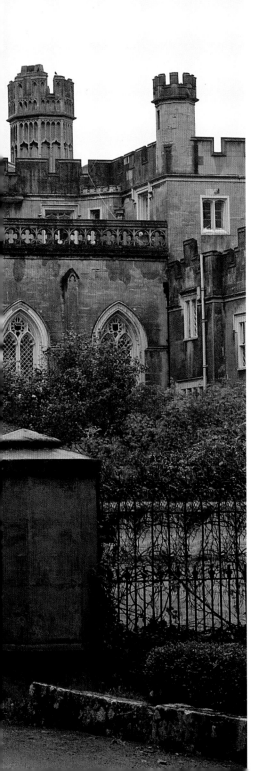

Conishead Priory, near Ulverston, would be astonishing wherever it was located, but in the setting of Lancashire north-of-the-sands it is even more unlikely. Designed in the Regency period, it is dramatic and unique, a flight of fancy in which gothic fantasy and outrageous expense run riot, not to say out of control – the result of a heady mix of money and eccentricity. It has been owned by the Manjushri Kadampa Meditation Centre since 1976.

The present Conishead Priory was built on the site of a twelfth-century Augustinian priory, which was a hospital with almshouses and domestic buildings. This area to the north of Morecambe Bay, also known as Furness, was monastic land. Furness Abbey, a few miles to the west in Barrow-in-Furness, was the second largest Cistercian house after Fountains Abbey in Yorkshire, with a vast amount of land extending as far as Coniston and Hawkshead, and bordering the land owned by Fountains up in the area of Grange-in-Borrowdale. Cartmel Priory lies a few miles to the east. The Augustinian Cartmel monks once had huge holdings in the southern reaches of what is now Cumbria.

The main church at Conishead is likely to have been located on what is now the south lawn, and carved sandstone blocks from the medieval chapter house can still be recognized in the south wall of the rebuilt priory.

The story of the present house begins in 1821. Colonel Braddyll's family had owned a sixteenth-century house on the site for over a hundred years, which he condescendingly described as a 'tolerable' dwelling, but once the colonel inherited it he decided that it was easier to rebuild than to repair a house for which he had little affection. Thanks to his coal fortune and a family history of ambitious marriages, Braddyll could afford to indulge himself and his wealth allowed him to build one of the unlikeliest buildings in Cumbria. He even hired his own hermit to live in the ruin on Chapel Island close by.

Seeking ostentation to the highest degree, Colonel Braddyll commissioned the architect Philip Wyatt (d.1835) to draw up plans. Philip was the youngest

Conishead Priory: the late gothic north front.

son of James Wyatt (1746–1813), the leading architect of the day. After his father's premature death in a carriage accident in 1813, while immersed in the creation of Belvoir Castle's gothic silhouette of towers and turrets, Philip continued to work on the castle, grasping the essentials of the gothic revival. His only other completed work is Wynyard Park in County Durham (1822–30) for the 3rd Marquess of Londonderry.

The building of the priory commenced in 1823, but by 1829 only half had been completed. Wyatt was sacked and work ground to a halt for some years. Wyatt was replaced by the firm of George Webster of Kendal in 1838. (In the 1830s Webster was also working on nearby Holker Hall – see page 102 – for the Duke of Devonshire.) By 1848 the priory was largely completed, the cost a staggering £149,000. Sadly, Braddyll was forced to sell his splendid creation after unwise speculation in the Durham coal mines tipped the balance of his finances and forced him to declare himself bankrupt. During the thirty years after the sale several owners came and went in quick succession, and a date of 1853 on the west wing indicates further building.

This period was followed by fifty years of stability after a Scottish syndicate recognized its potential as a hydropathic spa and purchased it in 1878. Known as 'The Paradise of Furness', the spa offered salt baths, lawn tennis and the delights of a seasonal resident orchestra. Soon establishing itself as the place to visit in the area, it operated successfully until 1928, when the Durham Miners' Welfare Committee took a forty-four-year tenure, interrupted only by the Second World War, when Conishead Priory became the north-west's largest military hospital.

When the miners' tenure ended in 1972, the contents had to be auctioned and the house's future was suddenly in the balance. Ideas for white-elephant buildings in the 1970s were hardly inspirational and the one carrying the most weight involved converting Conishead Priory into a holiday camp. Several years went by without a decision and the priory stood empty for what would be its most ruinous half-decade. Rainwater overflowing into the house from blocked gutters allowed dry rot to run rampant, reducing many of the structural timbers to powder. The priory teetered on the verge of demolition.

Salvation finally came via English Buddhists, in the form of the Manjushri Kadampa Meditation Centre, who secured it for £75,000 in 1976. The centre effectively bought a shell, and an unknown quantity of disintegration. One of its first priorities was to prop up the structural beams with felled trees from the woods, chemically treated to prevent recurrence of dry rot. The succeeding decades have witnessed a stewardship beyond expectation, and Conishead Priory has come full circle from ancient Augustinian priory through gothic revival fantasy to Buddhist religious retreat.

It appears that Philip Wyatt built the extensive corridor wing lit by five two-light windows (to the right of the soaring north entrance) and the Z-shaped service wing. The astounding asymmetrical late gothic north front (and former entrance) is George Webster's inspiration. Dame Edith Sitwell was once described as gothic enough to hang bells in, and much the same could be said of Colonel Braddyll's 'priory'. The gatehouse-type entrance, displaying a formidable collection of spires and lantern turrets amid a stone menagerie of carved animals, is sandwiched between twin towers 30 metres/100 feet

OPPOSITE The great hall awaits
renovation.
LEFT The cantilevered staircase
with carved badgers, emblems of
the Braddyll family.

FOLLOWING PAGES
ABOVE LEFT Braddyll coats of
arms punctuate the elaborate
plasterwork in the drawing room.
ABOVE RIGHT Exuberant
plasterwork in the saloon.
BELOW LEFT A Buddhist shrine.
BELOW RIGHT The cloistered
corridor.

tall. The ecclesiastically inspired windows along the north front do not merely punctuate the walls but appear to squeeze them to the edges.

The double-storey great hall appears to combine the baronial with the ecclesiastical, with a north-facing stained-glass window that would not be out of place in a cathedral. This would have been the entrance hall where guests were received; it was surely designed to make the visitor gape at its scale and magnificence. The hall is still in need of restoration; it is the last major area requiring attention, but the bones of the space are intact.

In keeping with the hall's lavish dimensions, the cloistered corridor and cantilevered staircase are scaled up to appear equally monumental. These main arteries of the house are practical spaces, but their location on the northern elevation means that light is at a premium. However, Wyatt's five generous two-light windows flying to the ceiling cause the light to dance all the way down the length of the corridor. Seemingly endless, the corridor stretches to an astonishing length and is one of the glories of the priory. Buddhist shrines have fitted seamlessly into the niches and their fluttering gaily coloured banners echo the heraldic details.

The windows on the half-landing are considered fine examples of early nineteenth-century work, comprising a set of three lights, steeped in manorial stained glass that proudly displays the Braddyll coats of arms, and those of families linked to them through ambitious marriage alliances. The Braddylls' self-importance is also indicated by the family's emblem of badgers rampant at the foot of the staircase.

1160	Gamelde Pennington founds a hospital overseen by the black canons of the Order of St Augustine.
1188	Raised to priory status in reign of Henry II (1154–89) in an attempt to raise profile and status with Furness Abbey.
1537	Dissolution of the Monasteries: the priory is seized by Crown under the Act of Suppression, and the lands then leased. Lead, bells, timber sold for £333 6s and 3d.
1540	Priory granted by Henry VIII to William Stanley, Lord Mounteagle
1548	The priory is bought by William Sandys of Colton Hall, an early iron master, brother of Archbishop Edwin Sandys.
1558	William Sandys, as Receiver General of Furness, becomes a victim of the local antagonism to the Crown and is murdered in a dispute.
1583	Francis Sandys, his son, dies without issue. Two married half-sisters inherit: Margaret Dodding and Barbara Philipson. Margaret's grandson, George Dodding, later buys out the Philipsons.
1683	His son, Miles Dodding, dies, leaving two daughters. One dies childless, so the estate passes through his sister, Sarah Braddyll, to her son, Dodding Braddyll. Thus the priory becomes a Braddyll seat, and remains so for almost two centuries.
1776	Thomas Braddyll, Dodding's son, dies unmarried. His first cousin once removed, Wilson Gale, inherits and becomes Wilson Gale-Braddyll.
1818	Thomas, his son, inherits and becomes Thomas Richmond-Gale-Braddyll, known as Colonel Braddyll.
1821	He becomes High Sheriff of Lancashire and the old house is demolished. Philip William Wyatt is commissioned to design a new house.
1829	Wyatt is dismissed with the house only half completed. Building work halted.
1835	Wyatt dies in the debtors' prison.
1838	George Webster of Kendal takes over.
1848	Having spent £149,000 on the building works Colonel Braddyll is declared bankrupt, after unwise speculation in the Durham coal mines.
1848–80s	A variety of different owners take possession.
1880s	The house becomes a luxurious hydropathic hotel, the Paradise of Furness.
1928	The Durham Miners' Welfare Committee miners' convalescent home buys the priory for £35,000 on a 44-year lease.
1940–45	The priory becomes the north-west's largest military hospital, with 8,000 in-patients over the years.
1950s	2,800 miners enjoy a two-week holiday here.
1972	The lease ends and the house and contents are auctioned. A bid to turn the site into a holiday camp fails and the threat of demolition looms.
1972–6	Conishead Priory lies abandoned and begins to deteriorate.
1976	The Manjushri Kadampa Meditation Centre purchase it for £75,000.
1980	The formerly derelict Conishead Priory becomes structurally secure.
1991	Appeal for £500,000 to complete building restoration and build accommodation.
1994	Over half this raised and the top-floor accommodation is finished.
2004	The Heritage Lottery Fund pledges £899,000 towards a £1.2m first phase of restoration work to replace slate roofs, fibreglass gutters, repair stonework and towers.

The formidable-looking staircase divides into two, which continue in the grand manner, eventually opening on to a gallery leading to several principal bedrooms. Every detail of the building works hard to represent a more glorious age, but the screen that separates the gallery overlooking the great hall is genuine seventeenth century from Salmesbury Hall, Preston.

The dining-room ceiling is one of the finest in the house. Today, its trestle tables and long benches give the room an institutional feel, but this reminds us that this is very much a hard-working, lived-in house, and the ceiling and the scale of the room still triumph. The linenfold carved oak wainscot panelling and the black marble fireplace are untouched. The mirror above the fireplace has replaced an enormous canvas.

The drawing room and saloon have been pressed into service as a sitting room and a sales area. Yet although these rooms have a contemporary look, the ornate plaster ceilings display the wonders of the original interior decoration. The saloon was the only area to escape dry rot in the 1970s, so remains the most original room in the house. The ceiling bears the arms of the Braddyll family; there is no escaping their sense of importance. The beautifully carved Carrara marble fireplace is a reminder that Colonel Braddyll bankrupted himself with this building.

Waterside settings are a recurring theme for some of Cumbria's most famous houses, and at Conishead the waters of Morecambe Bay lap against the peaceful shoreline of the estate; the bay makes a natural boundary. The 28 hectares/70 acres of garden and woodland include woodland walks with drifts of snowdrops, enormous rhododendrons and magnificent specimen trees.

The Manjushri Kadampa Meditation Centre runs Conishead Priory as an International Meditation Centre & Temple for World Peace, providing a place for daily prayers and meditation in the temple. The centre welcomes visitors to the priory, gardens and temple, to enjoy its conservatory café, and to join day or weekend courses and short retreats. Guided tours of the priory run during the season at the weekend and on bank holidays.

An active residential working visit programme encourages volunteers to become a part of the thriving community for a week. The setting establishes a reflective environment for a meaningful break and the programme is an introduction for those wishing to experience the Buddhist way of life first hand.

HUTTON-IN-THE-FOREST

'Forests ancient as the hills'

With many rooms unencumbered by the paraphernalia of the modern world, devoid of electricity and central heating, Hutton-in-the-Forest offers a view of the past unlike that of any other house in the county. The family dates back to Sir Richard Fletcher, who purchased the house in 1605. The house has been owned by the 2nd Baron Inglewood, Richard Fletcher Vane, and his wife, Cressida, since 1989, who have brought up their three children here.

On a first visit the house can seem overwhelming and almost confusing, such is the mixture of styles, for it is really three houses in one: a pele tower sandwiched between a 1630s gallery on its right and the east front of 1685 to its left.

Six different building periods define a span of five hundred years. The house emerges as an extravagant and whimsical mixture of seventeenth-century classical and nineteenth-century gothic romantic turrets and castellations.

The oldest part of the east-facing front elevation is a fourteenth-century pele tower, built by the de Hoton family, who gave Hutton its name, and like many pele towers, it was built as a defence against the Border reivers. At the beginning of the fourteenth century, Thomas de Hoton was Crown Forester when Hutton-in-the-Forest was one of the three principal manors of the royal forest of Inglewood, the second largest royal forest in England, covering much of what used to be the county of Cumberland in what is now north Cumbria. By the late sixteenth century the de Hotons' fortunes had changed, forcing them to sell up in 1605.

Richard Fletcher, a wealthy merchant from Cockermouth, purchased Hutton. Knighted by James I, he set about creating a suitably noble country house. Subsequently in the 1630s, his son, Sir Henry, 1st Baronet, built the second major addition, an impressive wing with a long gallery on the first floor above an open loggia, which has since been glassed in to become the tea room.

Hutton-in-the-Forest: from left to right, the Victorian south-east tower, the classical east front, the square pele tower, the sunlit long gallery and the Gladstone Tower.

FAR LEFT The south-east tower.
LEFT The pele tower's stone hall.
RIGHT The Cupid Staircase.
FAR RIGHT Salvin's hall with the
Cupid Staircase.

The third major addition was the classical east front built in 1685 by Sir Henry's son, Sir George Fletcher, 2nd Baronet. Quite unlike anything else in the county, this is the ornate façade in the centre of the east elevation, made with a pale limestone brought from the quarry at Lazonby. Its lightness of touch is emphasized by the muscularity and weight of the rest of the building surrounding it. It was built by Edward Addison to the design of William Talman.

The imposing south front dates from the beginning of the nineteenth century. This took shape in two stages. First, the architect Nixon of Carlisle created the neo-gothic lancet windows. He was followed by Anthony Salvin from 1820, and later during the 1860s to the 1880s, working in the medieval revival style. The character of the exterior, with its crenellated towers, owes much to him. Salvin had established a name for himself as an extender and remodeller of a large number of castles for wealthy Victorian patrons – in the 1850s he was heavily involved in the remodelling of Alnwick Castle in Northumberland, where he contrasted a gothic revival exterior with sumptuous Italian Renaissance-style interiors for the 4th Duke of Northumberland. Salvin would also be commissioned to remodel Muncaster Castle (see page 90).

The south-east tower dates from 1830. Salvin was commissioned with George Webster of Kendal to build an imposing neo-gothic tower which balances the pele tower, and on which the two dramatic elevations could pivot.

Finally in 1886 Margaret Gladstone, Lady Vane (a cousin of prime minister W.E. Gladstone), commissioned the Gladstone Tower on the north-east corner. Although it is little more than a conceit, it helps to balance the other two towers.

The cool barrel-vaulted stone hall at the base of the pele tower is the first of Hutton's two halls. Little in this central defensive stronghold seems to have changed since Hutton-in-the-Forest offered a refuge against the Border raiders in the mid-fourteenth century. The thick walls and barrel vaulting create an oppressive, dungeon-like feeling. Weaponry is decoratively displayed on the walls as the Victorians loved to arrange it.

Far more congenial a space can be found in the hall remodelled by Salvin in the 1830s. A heraldic and armorial atmosphere prevails, created by colourful coats of arms framed like noughts and crosses between the oak beams, a frieze of armour, antlers and swords above the oak panelling and a generous peppering of portraits.

Salvin retained the seventeenth-century panelling and the Cupid Staircase of the 1680s. The staircase dominates the short wall and upstages the huge fireplace soaring to the top of the panelling on the long wall. It is worth examining. The Italianate-style carving is of a high order and it is not often that you can examine cherubs at such close quarters, for they are normally suspended from the distant ceiling corners of double-storey rooms. In spite of their playful cavorting, these chubby figures are slightly gross and their angelic faces stare out in a disarming manner.

Salvin conjured up a neo-gothic extravaganza of a dining room, ripe with blues and reds, greys and browns. Superb generous floor-to-ceiling windows with doors on to the garden allow light to stream in from the south. Above the half-panelling, impressive ancestral canvases of the Vane family look down on the proceedings from a background of William Morris wallpaper. The recently commissioned contemporary chandelier, suitably baronial and well proportioned, shows how a period room can absorb modern work.

Hutton-in-the-Forest possesses two drawing rooms, both on the first floor but very different in character. The smaller of the two is early Georgian. Upon the death of the bachelor Sir Henry Fletcher, 3rd Baronet, in 1712, the baronetcy died out. His sister's son, Henry Vane Fletcher, eventually succeeded and in the 1740s created a suite of three Georgian rooms within the old pele tower. The suite comprises a drawing room, a dressing room and a bedroom.

The drawing room, known as the Cupid Room, is one of the most exquisite rooms in the county. Thought to have been designed by Daniel Garrett, an architect who worked on Savile Rowe, it takes its name from its inspired ceiling with a cupid in stucco plaster as its centrepiece. This delicate work was completed by one of Robert Adam's favourite plasterers, Joseph Rose 'the elder', for £25 in 1744. Compare this delicate cupid to the beefy cherubs on the Cupid Staircase in the hall. However, by 1874 the decoration had acquired a heavy Victorian decorative

scheme of blue, black and gold, since regarded as inappropriate for what must once have been intended as a light-hearted confection. Richard and Cressida Fletcher Vane asked Tim Mowl and Geoffrey Beard to return the partially destroyed scheme to its mid-eighteenth-century conception. Mowl and Beard realized that the north-west-facing aspect made it imperative to fill the room with as much light and as simple a scheme as possible, 'within the limits of mid-eighteenth-century authenticity'. Their colour theme pivots on four shades of biscuit, with the plaster relief highlighted in pure white. The refined simplicity has restored the strong eighteenth-century flavour. The room's clean lines are emphasized by balanced, elegant furnishings and an antique oriental rug contrasts with the sanded pine floorboards; every detail seems right.

The opulent drawing room in the south-east tower was built by George Webster of Kendal and improved by Salvin. Firmly of the nineteenth century, this main drawing room might be in a different house from the other one, so different is it in size, character and aspect. High south-facing gothic windows nudge the cornice and overlook the low garden and middle pond. Perhaps the design of the high thin-ribbed ceiling is meant to tie in with Hutton's long gallery of two centuries before. Although the room is Victorian, it is furnished in a light-hearted way, stopping short of nineteenth-century clutter. The Hepplewhite-style Gillow furniture, airy blue Morris wallpaper and brilliant yellow drapes give the room a Regency lightness of touch. Balanced picture hanging has long been an important consideration in the decoration of a house; here a contemporary painting of Richard and Cressida Fletcher Vane with their elder daughter, Miranda, sits comfortably near a George Romney portrait of Sir Frederick Fletcher Vane.

The long gallery is a splendid reminder of the great long galleries beloved of the Elizabethans and Jacobeans. When it was built over an open colonnade in the 1630s (the opening of Charles I's reign) the windows were placed on the north side, so as to overlook the walled garden; however, the room was restored in the nineteenth century and these windows were filled in, so now only the

OPPOSITE The dining room.
LEFT ABOVE The cupid ceiling in the Cupid Room.
LEFT BELOW The Cupid Room.

gazebo still offers an aerial view of the garden. Light streams through a bow window on the south side. The atmosphere of this room comes from the carved paneling, rows of family portraits, mainly of the Fletchers, and the fine range of Cumbrian court cupboards.

Hutton-in-the-Forest's library was once a drawing room and can be found in Addison's central late-seventeenth-century classical façade. The interior is late nineteenth century, dating from Anthony Salvin's commission, which led to the creation of oak bookcases, new oak doors and the ceiling.

The bedrooms comprise two of the suite of Georgian rooms, which includes the Cupid Room. The Blue Room, formerly a dressing room, appears as an authentic display, with fine eighteenth-century furniture. Nothing quite prepares you for the surprise that is Lady Darlington's Room, the effect exaggerated because you enter it straight after the two Georgian rooms. This is an unusual example of the Arts and Crafts style overlaying the bones of the original eighteenth-century room. William Morris wallpaper and green paint create an unmistakably Victorian atmosphere. The four-poster bed is made up from 'old' oak furniture. The room is named after a cousin, Caroline Lowther, who married Henry Vane, 2nd Earl of Darlington, a regular visitor in the second half of the eighteenth century.

The garden at Hutton-in-the-Forest is steeped in the past. The earliest terraces to the south and west date from the late seventeenth century, although Margaret, Lady Vane, embellished them with imposing topiary in the 1890s. The south terrace commands a view conceived by W.S. Gilpin in 1830 across a mid-eighteenth-century landscape.

ABOVE Lady Darlington's Room, in the style of William Morris.
RIGHT The long gallery has no rivals in the county.

Most of the summer colour can be found in the walled garden on the north side, the pattern of which can be seen from the gallery's gazebo. With an eye to growing fruit trees, two of the sides were walled in the 1730s by Henry Vane Fletcher. The rectangle was reconfigured by Margaret, Lady Vane, with her planting of the great yew hedges in the 1890s. Once a Victorian pleasure garden producing flowers, fruit and vegetables, the walled garden now enjoys a more serene atmosphere than hitherto. The rectangle is quartered to create compartments, and the accent is on double borders of herbaceous perennials, roses and trained fruit trees, which continue to smother the old walls. Oriental poppies are spectacular in June and in late summer several varieties of phlox provide colour for weeks.

The close proximity of two streams to the south and west inspired the creation of three ponds, the largest also being the oldest, dating back to the mid-eighteenth century, and stocked with fish for the table. Specimen trees, many planted in the early eighteenth century, are now a magnificent sight and determine the character of the garden.

Being a few miles north of the national park boundary, Hutton-in-the-Forest is slightly off the main tourist drag of the central Lakes, so the owners, Richard and Cressida Fletcher Vane, have had to be inventive and resourceful. Like many houses, Hutton divides its programme into recurring and annual events. Gamekeeper's walks, meet-the-gardener walks and horse trials are recurring fixtures. School trips are encouraged and children are welcome to enjoy historic tours, sketching in the walled garden and the woodland walks.

Hutton's parkland lends itself to large-scale outside events and with the fairytale backdrop of the house it makes a most congenial setting. The Near Park and Far Park both host annual events. The season also includes a plant and food fair in May and the Lakeland Historic Vehicle Show in June. Potfest in the Park, which celebrates Lady Inglewood's enthusiasm for ceramics, and the Skelton Show are both popular occasions in July. Open-air theatre performances, special receptions and concerts in the house complete the picture.

Richard and Cressida Fletcher Vane have been the owners of Hutton-in-the-Forest since 1989, and have been quietly getting on with ensuring that the place is in good order ever since. Making sure that 'the lid is on the tin' – that the roof is in an acceptable state of repair – was the first priority. Whenever work needs carrying out, their aim has always been to fix it properly in the hope that it will last for more than a century. Meanwhile, reinstating the nineteenth-century landscape to the south of the castle is an ongoing project for the next decade.

ABOVE The walled garden.
BELOW Potfest in the Park.

1292	Edward I visits the house owned by the de Hotons, one of three principal manors in royal forest of Inglewood.
***c.*1350**	The pele tower is built to defend the de Hotons from Scots.
1605	The de Hotons sell to the Cockermouth merchant Richard Fletcher (knighted by James I), who begins the conversion to a country house.
1630s	His son, Sir Henry, created a baronet, adds the gallery.
1680s	Sir George, his son, 2nd Bt, adds the classical east front, built by Addison and possibly designed by Talman. Sir George's daughter, Catherine Fletcher, marries Lyonel Vane, the son of Sir George Vane, whose elder brother Sir Harry Vane, prominent parliamentarian and secretary to Admiralty Board in Commonwealth, was executed for treason in 1662.
LATE 17THC	Terraces are created to the south and west.
1700	Catherine's father, Sir George Fletcher, dies, succeeded by his unmarried, childless eldest son, Sir Henry, 3rd Bt.
1712	Sir Henry's cousin, Thomas Fletcher, succeeds.
1730s	The garden is walled on two sides to grow fruit trees.
1732	His nephew, Henry Vane Fletcher, second son of Lyonel and Catherine, succeeds and improves the garden, grounds and estate. He does not marry.
1740s	Henry Vane Fletcher builds the Cupid Room, the Blue Room and Lady Darlington's Room, all by Daniel Garrett. The Middle Pond and Cascade are made.
1745	The house is occupied in the Scots Rebels' Invasion.
1761	Henry's younger brother, Walter, succeeds.
1775	Walter's son, Lyonel, succeeds. Created a baronet in 1786, he reverts to the Vane surname.
1786	Sir Lyonel's eldest son, Sir Frederick, 2nd Bt, succeeds and his huntsman John Peel breaks the record for foxhunting in 1830s with a 70-mile run.
EARLY 19THC	The south façade is altered by Nixon of Carlisle, introducing round headed windows.
1820s	Sir Frederick's son, Sir Francis, 3rd Bt, succeeds, and with his wife, Diana Olivia, restores, extends and renovates the house, employing George Webster of Kendal and Anthony Salvin, who produces plans for south-east Tower *c.*1830 and the castellations.
1842	After the early death of Sir Francis, Sir Henry, 4th Bt, succeeds, aged twelve. Further worked is carried out to house.
1860–80	The south front by Anthony Salvin is added. Romantic castle outline created by Salvin for south-east tower for Sir Henry. The Stone Hall at base of pele tower is turned into the main entrance.
1890s	Yew topiary hedges bound the remaining two sides of the walled garden. The south terraces and middle pond are remodelled by William Sawrey Gilpin.
1886	Gladstone tower built by Sir Henry's wife Margaret Gladstone.
1908	The estate is held in trust after Sir Henry dies without issue.
1931	A cousin, William Vane, succeeds, and takes the surname Fletcher Vane. (He is a direct descendant of Sir Henry Vane the Younger, executed in 1662.)
1945	William Vane is elected MP for Westmorland.
1964	William Vane is created Lord Inglewood.
1989	His elder son, Richard, former MEP, succeeds, as 2nd Lord Inglewood. Richard and his brother, Christopher, were the first children to be born in the house for over a hundred years.

MUNCASTER CASTLE

'Midway on the waves'

Located on Cumbria's west coast and boasting a romantic promontory setting as fine as any in Europe, the stronghold of Muncaster enjoys a commanding view towards Scafell Pike, the highest summit in England. Its setting on a spur above the river Esk and its estuary makes it the most notable landmark in the area. The Pennington family have owned the castle since 1208. Phyllida and Patrick Gordon-Duff-Pennington inherited the castle in 1982. They handed over the reins to their daughter Iona and son-in-law Peter Frost-Pennington, who is now managing director.

Muncaster Castle has always been remote. The road has to avoid the fells and meanders to say the least, and anyone approaching from the shore was dependent on the tides – the bridge over the river was only erected in 1828. Muncaster has one of the most famous gardens in the county, in an unrivalled location: it overlooks a ghyll bursting with azaleas and rhododendrons, punctuated by mature specimens of purple-leaved Japanese maples – a scene that could almost be a Himalayan ravine. The terrace walk offers a magnificent panorama of the western fells.

Although the castle dates from 1208, what we see today is mostly Anthony Salvin's neo-medieval red granite reconstruction with red sandstone dressings. His remodelling of the castle dates from 1862: he was commissioned by the 4th Lord Muncaster in the early 1860s and returned for a commission from the 5th Lord a decade later in 1872.

When Salvin arrived, he found a four-storey pele tower and a long range of a medieval house, plus an earlier reconstruction dating from the eighteenth century built by the 1st Lord Muncaster, which included a

The granite austerity of Anthony Salvin's reconstruction suits the remote western Lake District.

double-storey octagonal library, a kitchen tower and south-facing loggia. Leaving the pele tower and original medieval building, Salvin set to work. He gave the library a square tower complete with battlements, built a kitchen tower and improved the symmetry by creating a south-west service tower to balance the north-west pele tower. The loggia was demolished to make way for a progression of state rooms and he roofed in a courtyard to create the drawing room.

Salvin's genius was to capitalize on the location, striving for romantic effect and largely succeeding. The standard of workmanship is so high that it is not easy to differentiate Salvin's work from the masonry of the 1st Lord's time. After Salvin had worked his magic, Muncaster emerged looking splendidly rugged: a proud crenellated silhouette of granite towers and battlements that studs the skyline, with sandstone mullioned and transomed windows.

The hall is the original great hall and part of the medieval stronghold. Phyllida and Patrick Gordon-Duff-Pennington recall dining here in her grandfather's time and the hall has a strong Victorian atmosphere, overflowing with items from a massive collection. Acknowledging that this room is an essential part of their lives, the owners charmingly confess to finding it difficult to keep a sense of order, and worry about the wear and tear on the floor, and the heating. One of their least-loved relations, Sir Joseph Pennington, 4th Baronet, glares down on the family

dogs, who remain indifferent to the 'please do not touch' labels on the chairs. Meanwhile the family refers to the portrait of Henry VI over the library door as 'awful'.

Just outside the library door there are two part-sets of blue and gold Sèvres services, pre-Revolution of 1780, but only decorated in 1821. They were found by Phyllida's mother in a box marked 'broken china' down in the cellar. The statue by John of Bologna, known as the 'Alabaster Lady', has been placed so as to catch the afternoon sunlight. This is enhanced by a west-facing English stained-glass window at the foot of the staircase, dating from 1520, with the typical yellows and browns of that period.

On the staircase three exquisite Canova marbles of around 1810, which were originally meant to be set in the wall, are framed in wood. Patrick Gordon-Duff-Pennington comments that when the roof needs its next major overhaul, they can be removed easily and sold to pay for it if times are hard.

Muncaster Castle is stuffed with the improbable. Look out for the case containing the Star of Ethiopia presented in 1914 by Emperor Haile Selassie to Sir William Pennington as a boy for demonstrating how a lawnmower worked.

Muncaster's dining room shares similarities with the dining room at Levens Hall. While admiring the glistening combination of gold leaf and antique leather above the half-panelling remodelled by Salvin, you will recall the Cordova leather walls at Levens. And the county seems

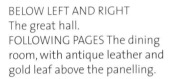
BELOW LEFT AND RIGHT
The great hall.
FOLLOWING PAGES The dining room, with antique leather and gold leaf above the panelling.

LEFT The drawing room.
RIGHT The octagonal library.

to be well endowed with rare Charles II walnut chairs, for there are a dozen more here, as at Levens. The collection of Derby plates of 1821 was soon lost after 1825. Once it was discovered a few years ago, the collection was lent to an exhibition at Burlington House, and unfortunately while it was still on loan several were accidentally damaged. Patrick Gordon-Duff-Pennington rejoices that they have been restored so brilliantly that the damage is imperceptible.

Several of the paintings have interesting tales behind them. Over the fireplace is Gainsborough's copy of Titian's *The Vendramin Family* in the National Gallery, which he painted for a bet. Looking down from above a recess over the sideboard is the *Study of a Boy with Falcon*: this was once thought to be by Velásquez, but has now been investigated by at least five experts who have all come up with a different painter. A hidden Bible drawer in the top of the walnut cabinet was a necessary precaution for Protestants after the St Bartholomew's Day Massacre of 1572 when French Catholics massacred 13,000 Protestants. Protestants believed in open access to the Bible, but Catholics considered it a dangerous book unless interpreted by priests.

Salvin closed in the old courtyard to create the drawing room. Its high coved ceiling is enlivened with delicate plasterwork and its height allows portraits to be hung in a two-tier arrangement. The white late eighteenth-century marble fireplace is from Bulstrode, and displays Apollo and Diana flanking the opening, with Apollo and the nine Muses on the lintel. Patrick Gordon-Duff-Pennington is proud of the figure of a stag, a retirement gift from the estate staff, which is inscribed 'for annoying those who needed it'. He feels it says much about how he has carried out his affairs over the years.

The double-storey octagonal library is one of the most exciting rooms in the house. The original library was begun in 1780 on the site of the medieval kitchens, its ceiling decorated with signs of the Zodiac. Salvin completed the room in its final form in 1862. Although any suggestion of heat disappears instantly into the celestial gothic vault above, the library has often been used as the family sitting room. Back in the early 1980s before natural gas had been connected, Phyllida and Patrick Gordon-Duff-Pennington would huddle here in sleeping bags

on winter evenings, perhaps wondering what on earth they had let themselves in for. Pennington family portraits stare down from above the gallery; the present owners note ruefully that they are somewhat inferior to those painted of the Ramsden side of the family. Look out for the Crimean travelling chest of curious bottled potions and Dr Brodum's *Guide to Old Age*.

The two notable bedrooms are the King's Room and the West Bedroom. The King's Room panelling and carving dates from the sixteenth century. The carving of St Francis in the canopy of the bed is a highlight, and the tiles in the grate made by William de Morgan are worth noting. The oldest artefact in the family's possession is the commode, which is reputed to have been in the possession of Henry VI's Gentleman of the Bedchamber.

In pride of place in the haunted West Bedroom is a richly carved Elizabethan four-poster bed, inlaid with bog oak and holly, which were popular timbers of the period, also seen at Sizergh Castle. At the end of the passage is a portrait of Thomas Skelton, manager and 'the last Fool of Muncaster', upon whom Shakespeare modelled the character in *King Lear*. We have to thank Skelton for the word 'tomfoolery'.

The hundreds of rhododendrons in the landscape at Mancaster inspired John Ruskin to describe it as the 'Gateway to Paradise'. The castle's commanding view over the borrowed landscape of Scafell Pike and the western fells dominates the outlook, especially from the Georgian terrace. A stroll along this terrace between April and June to absorb the view and the rich plantings has to be one of Cumbria's greatest treats, if not the British Isles'. Plants and a keen sense of place fuse together seamlessly, as if the exotic plantings have always been here. Plants luxuriate as if they were in Cornwall, in a garden that once held the largest collection of species rhododendrons in Europe.

For a garden that is planted with so many large-leaved evergreens, which struggle in the teeth of the prevailing westerly winds racing in off the Irish Sea, some serious groundwork had to be done. As long ago as the 1780s John, 1st Lord Muncaster, was busy planting a shelterbelt

of hardwood trees. By the 1840s the first rhododendrons were being planted and added to by the botanist Joseph Hooker, with collections from Sikkim, including his star discovery, *Rhododendron arboreum*, which varies in colour from bridal white to blood red.

Sir John Ramsden inherited Muncaster in 1917. He already possessed a fine rhododendron garden, Bulstrode in Gerrards Cross, Buckinghamshire, and quickly recognized that the Gulf Stream influence and acid soil made Muncaster one of the best places in Britain to cultivate the rhododendron seedlings he wished to transplant to the north. One of his original ideas was to save the best of the many new hybrids he was working on, but his achievements in this field were curtailed by the shortage of labour in 1939. This resulted in specimens shaded by the unmanaged beech trees becoming leggy and eventually ceasing to flower. Sadly, some of the trees are now nearing maturity after more than two hundred years.

In addition to the rhododendrons, camellias, magnolias, hydrangeas and maples flourish in the 31 hectares/77 acres of mature woodland. Various species of nothofagus, the southern beech, which grows in the southern hemisphere, also thrive. Muncaster owes much to the travels of George Forrest and Frank Kingdon-Ward, who explored remote mountainous areas in the Sino-Himalayan region of China in quest of plants and seeds. It was their pioneering work that led to this large collection of 'captive plants' in cultivation, guaranteeing their survival in the face of the continuing alarming deforestation in that area.

Serious garden restoration work began in the mid-1990s, and several miles of choked paths have become usable once more. The garden is now maintained by the head gardener, two gardeners and a forester.

Muncaster Castle's location on the west coast removes it from the beaten track (it is not within twenty minutes of a motorway). The scenic drive there is not on the quickest road in Cumbria, but once reached the castle and grounds are infinitely rewarding. The challenge for the

Pennington family lies in tempting people away from the central Lakes and the more accessible regions of the county. This means highlighting the peaceful quieter coastline and 'Britain's favourite view' – that of Great Gable reflected at the head of Wastwater. There is a further catch, however: Muncaster's gardens are its glory, yet a limitation because of the high proportion of azaleas and rhododendrons. The garden looks fabulous for three months and it is one of the must-see gardens in the county, and indeed the north-west, but come the end of June, inevitably the garden has peaked. With a preponderance of spring- and early summer-flowering shrubs there is not much space in which to integrate perennial borders which could make their mark until October.

Muncaster is run by the managing director, Peter Frost-Pennington, and his wife, Iona, daughter of Phyllida and Patrick Gordon-Duff-Pennington. If Iona's parents once saw the castle as their home with a business attached, Peter recognizes that the situation is now the reverse, with the family playing the role of stewards and custodians. A paramount commitment is to make visitors feel at home and continue the tradition that this is a much-loved family home with a congenial atmosphere looking positively to the future. One of Muncaster's great selling points is the size and scale of the castle and its gardens and grounds. Even on a busy day, there is plenty of space if you wander from the main throng of activity; peace and tranquillity are never far away. Peter is finding that the availability of online ticketing on the castle's website helps them anticipate visitor numbers and commits people to their day out as if they had booked a theatre or cinema ticket.

No one would venture to suggest that Muncaster Castle has not been inventive. Virtually anything is possible here. The shroud of late winter is torn open by a February half-term opening. The season proper kicks off on 1 April with the annual Festival of Fools, at which Thomas Skelton, the late Fool (jester) of Muncaster, is honoured. (There must be something in the air around here, as Wasdale holds a 'biggest liar in the world competition' in November. This recalls the tall tales told by nineteenth-century Cumbrian publican Will Riston, known as 'Auld Will'.) A Feast of Flowers runs from late April to early May. In October Hallowe'en ghost tours threaten to scare visitors to death. Darkest Muncaster sound and light shows of the garden's trees and shrubs offer a mystical winter experience. Christmas is celebrated with special openings to view the decorations and Victorian house tours with guides in costume on Sundays.

The World Owl Centre here allows visitors to adopt an owl, and falcon displays take place every afternoon in the season. Civil ceremonies and wedding breakfasts are held in the castle and evening parties in one of the courtyard's function rooms. Muncaster hosts a variety of events from corporate occasions for up to a hundred to team-building events. It also runs a Friends' scheme, offering free access to the gardens and discounts at various castle facilities. The Old Dairy offers twelve accessible workstations, open to visitors most afternoons. Schools are offered history tours, and in addition to the castle being a popular draw for primary schools, efforts have been made to tie the tours in with the national curriculum in geography, science and history.

Muncaster Castle is in much better shape than it was when Phyllida and Patrick Gordon-Duff-Pennington anxiously took over the helm in 1982, with a £50,000 loss running for five years. In spite of all their enterprising efforts, by 1995 there were no funds in the bank, which forced the creation of the

1208	Lands are granted to Alan de Penitone.
1258	The castle is built by Gamel de Mulcastre.
14THC	The pele tower is erected on Roman foundations.
1464	Sir John Pennington shelters the fugitive Henry VI. Legend reveals that as long as the drinking bowl the king presented to Sir John, known as the Luck of Muncaster, remains unbroken, the Penningtons should live and thrive at Muncaster.
1783 ONWARDS	There is a vacancy in the Irish peerage and the 5th Baronet is created 1st Baron Muncaster, who carries out extensive renovations, including the library and erects a tower to commemorate Henry VI. Most of the estate's large hardwood trees are planted.
1862–6 AND 1872–4	Anthony Salvin is engaged to rebuild house.
1880s	C. J. Ferguson continues work on house and creates a billiard room, 1886.
1917	The last Lord Muncaster dies and estate reverts to Ramsdens.
1920–58	In the garden Sir John Ramsden plants rhododendron seedlings, together with fine collection of magnolia, camellia, maple and hydrangea.
1982	Patrick and Phyllida Gordon-Duff-Pennington make Muncaster their permanent home, which is now run by their daughter Iona and son-in-law Peter Frost-Pennington.

Muncaster is home to the World
Owl Centre.

Third Millennium Muncaster Project. By the end of 2000 the £5.5 million required had been raised, with the Millennium Commission raising 50 per cent and the balance contributed by the Pennington family, English Heritage, the Headlye Trust, the EU, the Rural Development Commission and countless donations from local businesses, individuals and organizations.

In 1996 the roof was completely repaired and the dry rot eradicated. The gardens have been restored beyond all recognition, and Royal Horticultural Society tours now take place when the gardens are at their peak. Some of the money raised by the Penningtons involved the sale of several items, including a set of the English Romantic painter Thomas Girtin's watercolours discovered in a folder among some stored linen. Girtin (1775–1802) was a gifted contemporary of Turner, and might have eclipsed him had he lived. In 1997 internal refurbishments included environmentally sensitive heating, and new kitchen and toilet facilities to allow the hosting of weddings, corporate events and celebrations all year round.

Iona and Peter Frost-Pennington are optimistic about the future. Peter realizes the house's potential and is a fast-talking powerhouse of ideas, fluent with today's rapidly changing technology. The restored rooms around the courtyards have blank walls facing the castle; he would love to introduce the odd window so that visitors, be they conference delegates or wedding guests, could enjoy that view. He also favours a better link with the railway. Muncaster's future appears to be in safe and enthusiastic hands.

HOLKER HALL

'A stately pleasure-dome'

Holker Hall, near Grange-over-Sands, is a spacious and airy house with light-filled rooms and a charismatic atmosphere, in the setting of the outlying Cumbrian fells and Morecambe Bay. Once owned by the Dukes of Devonshire, the house is now the home of Lord and Lady Cavendish.

The house stands on land owned by Cartmel Priory until the Dissolution of the Monasteries in 1536. After the dissolution, the Preston family wished to add to their extensive local estates and purchased this land, finally making Holker their home from around 1610. Holker later passed into the hands of the Lowther family until 1756. Holker began its connection with the Cavendish family when Sir Thomas Lowther married the 2nd Duke of Devonshire's daughter, Lady Elizabeth Cavendish, in the early eighteenth century. Holker then became a popular Cumbrian retreat for several Dukes of Devonshire. Upon the death of the 8th Duke of Devonshire in 1908, Holker was inherited by the second son, Lord Richard, rather than the 9th Duke. It then ceased to be in the ownership of the Dukes of Devonshire. The present owner, Hugh Cavendish, is Lord Richard's grandson.

The Prestons' original house was extended or refaced over the centuries until, inspired by George Webster's work at Conishead Priory a few miles away (see page 74), the 6th Duke of Devonshire commissioned Websters of Kendal to rebuild the eighteenth-century hall in the Jacobean style between 1838 and 1842, transforming the house with two impressive wings. Mullioned and transomed windows, a multitude of ornate chimneys and steep gables gave the house a Jacobean appearance. However, less than thirty years later, on 9 March 1871, the entire west wing was gutted by fire. Valuable treasures were lost and there was no choice but to rebuild. By this time the 6th Duke had died and Holker had passed to his grandson, William Cavendish, the 7th Duke, who commissioned the Lancaster architects Paley & Austin.

Holker Hall: Paley & Austin's west wing is in the Elizabethan style, yet remains quintessentially Victorian.

Paley & Austin were primarily ecclesiastical architects in the north-west – the remodelling of St Martin's Church in Bowness is a good example of their work – but they also designed several notable railway stations on the Furness line, including that at nearby Grange-over-Sands, and the west wing of Leighton Hall near Carnforth in 1870. Prior to these commissions, the partners Edmund Sharpe and E.G. Paley were known for flowing tracery and churches in terracotta. When Sharpe retired in 1851, Paley took H.J. Austin into the business and it was he who designed the firm's masterpieces. Paley's son joined in 1890 and Paley himself died five years later, after which the firm became known as Austin & Paley until the 1930s.

With inspired alchemy, Paley & Austin presented an unmistakably Victorian house that overflows with the confidence and prosperity of the era but glories in the Elizabethan style, harking back to that golden age of building activity in the county. The craftsmanship is superb and the firm probably surpassed the 7th Duke's expectations, turning red sandstone imported from Runcorn in Cheshire into a staggering display of Elizabethan motifs, all conspiring to dazzle and impress. No grand house was built without an element of bravura, and ducal Holker positively swaggers. The imposing Victorian architecture is redolent of the central buildings of the great northern cities, which seem to have been transplanted to a favoured spot on Morecambe Bay.

Paley & Austin's west wing, completed in 1874, runs roughly on a north–south axis. The long east-facing front elevation boasts an imposing four-storey square tower reminiscent of a pele tower, although the concept of a defensive building had been long redundant.

The western garden elevation, filled with mullioned and transomed windows, is relieved by several jutting bays and irregularly placed dormers, their steep gables breaking up the roofline. This asymmetrical appearance, exaggerated by the bulk of the square tower and separate cupola, is made even more jagged by thrusting chimneystacks competing as to which can soar the highest.

On the gable end of the southern elevation a triangular oriel window, with a pair of matching dormers almost in the centre, is impressive but the focal point, shared with the west elevation, is the double-storey circular corner bay, the curved windows of which flood the drawing room and the Duke's Bedroom with light.

The original Webster wing, running at right angles to the Paley & Austin wing and screened by the private gardens, continues to be lived in by the Cavendishes and it is to the 'new' west wing with its state rooms that today's visitors are welcomed. Although the state rooms in a grand house were not designed to be used on a daily basis, Hugh Cavendish's grandparents were living in this wing until the outbreak of the Second World War and today's absence of ropes continues to give the impression of a family home in daily use.

Floor-to-ceiling limestone archways dominate the entrance hall. The limestone was quarried on the estate at nearby Stainton and polished to resemble marble. The archways indicate the route to the generous cantilever staircase beyond, dripping with Elizabethan-style pendants. Each of the hundred closely spaced carved balusters marching upwards is unique, thought to be designed by J.G. Crace. The eighteenth-century rent table was still in use in 1914.

The heraldic past is celebrated in the north-facing stained-glass windows with the ducal coronet and monogram of the 7th Duke of Devonshire and the coats of arms

arms of the Clifford, Cavendish and Lowther families. The often repeated snake is a Cavendish family emblem and the punning motto *Cavendo tutus* is best translated as 'Look before you leap'.

The hall's excellent acoustics have made it a convivial room for fund-raising concerts in aid of the charities that Holker supports. Guests arriving on winter evenings have to use a different entrance, as the front door has to remain firmly shut; this reminds the present owner, Hugh Cavendish, of draughty days when he was a boy and you could always count on a strategically placed forest of screens wherever you looked. As a visitor showing admission tickets before heading off for the library, it is easy to miss the detail of this room, but the hall offers a superb introduction to the high quality of craftsmanship throughout. The oak half-panelling depicts beautifully carved local flora and fauna. The upper walls of stone create a monumental atmosphere and lead the eye upwards to the ornate white plaster ceiling.

A carved inscription on the mantelpiece above the sandstone fireplace records the date of the fire on 9 March 1871 and the completion of the rebuilding in 1874. Poignant reminders of the many fine objects destroyed in the blaze are the few marble fragments embedded in the surround of the marble fireplace inset within the larger one: these were saved from a pedestal that crumbled to the touch after the fire. The exquisite Victorian craftsmanship of the entire 'new' wing is all the more astonishing when you consider that it took a mere three years for this enormous building to rise like a phoenix from the ashes.

Bacchus is rhapsodized in the dining room and the lavish treatment of the fireplace makes it the focal point of the room. Carved grape vines twining around two pairs of estate-grown spiralled oak columns shoot up almost to the ceiling. Further grapes and fruits are framed in the half-panelling. Eternally imprisoned in their frames, portraits of the Cavendishes and Lowthers gaze from the walls with indifferent stares, while a self-portrait of van Dyck is given pride of place over the fireplace. The Delft tiles in the fireplace came from the Duke of Devonshire's seat at Chatsworth in Derbyshire.

Since even the idea of thirty-two indoor servants has become remote, Hugh Cavendish comments that whenever he and his wife, Grania, host a dinner party, most of the evening evaporates in marching hither and thither. This has been exacerbated since the conversion of the old kitchens into flats, making the new kitchen even more remote. In the 1970s the family would usually showcase the Christmas tree in the dining room and have lunch for thirty-five to forty in the hall.

The drawing rooms of Muncaster Castle and Holker Hall are only a decade apart. Holker's is sumptuous yet comfortable, inviting and appropriately grand, as befitting the 7th Duke of Devonshire. The architects Paley & Austin employed the firm of J.G. Crace to decorate the interior and they rose to the challenge in the grand style. With walls covered in red Macclesfield silk to complement the paintings, the room comes into its own at dusk, when the recessed lighting above the cornice adds an inviting glow. Intertwining leaves and linenfold panelling add a luxurious touch to the oak half-panelling.

ABOVE The entrance hall with its limestone arches. An inscription above the fireplace notes the date of the fire of 1871.
BELOW The dining room, with van Dyck's self-portrait above the fireplace and spiralled columns of estate-grown oak.

LEFT ABOVE The drawing room with ornate Elizabethan-style ceiling.
LEFT BELOW The library, with Sir William Richmond's portrait of Lady Frederick Cavendish above the fireplace.
BELOW The billiards room.

The Carrara marble fireplace was bought for £168 by Lady Louisa, the 7th Duke's daughter, from Montague House in London in 1874. Its overmantel looking-glass soaring to the cornice reflects the light from the corner bay window and highlights the intricate plaster ceiling. With its elegant Louis XV and Louis XVI furniture and deep Hepplewhite sofas, the room achieves what Gervase Jackson-Stops described as that 'peculiarly English mixture of grandeur and informality, together with a balanced asymmetry in the arrangement of the furniture' redolent of Chatsworth.

The library is one of Holker's most engaging rooms. With west-facing floor-to-ceiling bay windows it feels bright even on dull days and has pleasant views of the garden. Derbyshire alabaster fireplaces inlaid with Italian marble at opposite ends of the room ensure that when fires are lit anyone immersed in the books here would never get chilled. The tall oak bookcases, segmented with pilasters and topped with a generous carved cornice, glow with carefully concealed lighting fitted in 1911. The switches are hidden behind a run of faux books with preposterously waggish titles and authors.

Fortunately many of the books were saved from the fire of March 1871. The library contains 3,500 volumes, including volumes originating from Chatsworth. On one occasion when HRH Prince Philip was staying at Holker, there was a chimney fire in the Webster wing, where the family live. The library had to be pressed into service as a sitting room with both its fires lit. Although the state rooms are not used on a regular basis, it was soon evident how much a well-designed Victorian house lends itself to entertaining.

Leisure and exercise go hand in hand in the billiards room at Holker Hall. The original interior decoration was again by J.G. Crace. The superb wood carving here and elsewhere at Holker, inspired by flower, leaf and berry, anticipates Baillie Scott's illustration of the local natural world in the carving at Blackwell (see page 114) by thirty years. When the room had to be redecorated, Grania Cavendish and decorator Caroline Gibbs hand-stencilled the room with eight layers of paint to create a wonderful depth, lustre and vitality. Now, the sumptuous finish ensures that a game of billiards has a great deal to live up to.

ABOVE LEFT The Duke's Bedroom, located over the drawing room.
ABOVE RIGHT Queen Mary's Bedroom, named after the queen's visit in 1937.
RIGHT The Duke's Bedroom affords a fine view of the garden's structure.

The first-floor gallery is a Victorian variation of the familiar long narrow gallery found in the great Elizabethan houses. Located above the entrance hall, the gallery faces north, yet the run of almost floor-to-ceiling windows makes this a very light space. Twin polished limestone arches similar to the ones in the hall are repeated at the staircase end. Flamboyant William Morris patterned wallpaper enliven the walls above the half-panelling.

The Duke's Bedroom is the finest bedroom. Of all the Devonshire houses, which included Chatsworth, Hardwick Hall, Londesborough Hall, Lismore Castle, Chiswick House and their London houses, the 7th Duke, William, preferred Holker and his monogram reminds us that this was his bedroom up until his death in 1891.

The craftsmanship is a joy to behold. The panelling combines natural as well as bleached oak and the elaborate plasterwork ceiling shows Paley & Austin celebrating a key detail of a great Elizabethan house. The room has been redecorated by Grania Cavendish: the pale wallpaper of the post-war redecoration has been swept away in favour of a rich red wallpaper, which echoes the lining of the half-tester and the cloak and apron on display and repeats the geometric symmetry of the ceiling pattern. The captivating aerial view of the gardens and park through the circular corner bay window has been made more absorbing in recent years by Hugh and Grania Cavendish's gradual addition of evergreen structural interest in the form of topiary and clipped Portuguese laurel arches.

Queen Mary's Bedroom, named as a reminder of Her Majesty's visit in 1937, is a lighter and more feminine room, which also enjoys fine south-facing views of the garden. Recent redecoration, honouring the spirit of the original style with William Morris bed hangings, curtains and chair covers, has created a comfortable and satisfying unity.

Holker Hall enjoys a favoured location on one of the most southerly tips of the Lake District peninsulas, protected from the Irish Sea by Morecambe Bay. You could be forgiven for thinking that a Cumbrian outpost might be a bleak place in which to garden, but this stretch of coastline enjoys a microclimate, benefiting from the influence of the Gulf Stream, mild winters and an ample rainfall of approximately 112 centimetres/44 inches per annum. Big-leaved rhododendrons flourish here but the threat of late spring frosts on blooms is a constant worry. The flowers of magnolias towering to tree height can disintegrate overnight, but the garden is sheltered enough by mature trees for a wide spectrum of spring-flowering shrubs to be able to grow. These plants often look at their best when enhanced by the light; the quality of the light around Morecambe Bay is peculiarly brilliant.

In the nineteenth century Joseph Paxton redesigned certain areas of the garden with the 7th Duke (Paxton also worked at Chatsworth). Over the decades Holker has become noted for its collection of specimen trees, which enjoy the climate here. Some have been grown from seed, such as the cedar of Lebanon and the group of monkey puzzles (*Araucaria araucana*). The original monkey puzzle, planted in 1844 and still going strong, blew down after forty years but was righted with the aid of seven shire horses before having its roots embedded in concrete. The Holker lime, 8 metres/26 feet in girth, is one of fifty trees around the country chosen to mark the Queen's Jubilee celebrations.

Much of the essential groundwork for the gardens was laid down in the early twentieth century by the Devonshire family's keen plantswomen. Hugh Cavendish recalls how his great-aunt, Lady Evelyn Fitzmaurice, planted the cypress trees and had the fountain installed. His grandmother, Lady Moyra Cavendish, planted scores of rare trees and shrubs, which have since matured.

However, those green-fingered ladies could never have foreseen the changes to society forced by both world wars. Before 1914 there were eighteen full-time gardeners; now there are four. Life was even more different by the end of the Second World War and in 1945 Hugh Cavendish's mother, Pamela, had much to occupy her. Post-war conditions forced the garden to stand still for many years. The pattern of life among the landed gentry with its distinct social movements was also an influence. Hugh Cavendish's forebears would have embarked on the London season as soon as spring was over, so there was little concept of a summer garden, as the family was seldom in residence.

Since 1972, when Hugh and Grania Cavendish inherited Holker Hall, there has been an ongoing programme of change. Hugh Cavendish is a shrubs and trees man and Grania Cavendish is an artistic plantswoman, and their different enthusiasms and priorities have merged to create much of the present garden. They have discovered that they prefer working by instinct from the standpoint of whether a plant will be happy in the location they have decided for it. They have also been keen to absorb the landscape beyond. Instead of being satisfied with the inward-looking feel of an enclosed formal garden they have opened up vistas to absorb the wider landscape.

In the last twenty years, though, they have returned to a more formal style of gardening with an emphasis on structure. The level areas around the hall contain formal enclosures with box-edged compartments of bulbs and perennials, created by Hugh and Grania. The first two enclosures, the Elliptical Garden and the Summer Garden, rely on box, yew, clipped hawthorn standards and a tunnel of glossy-leaved Portuguese laurel, broken by a circle with quadrant beds leading to a round pond. The tunnel started as a double row of laurel standards but the clutter of bobbles was too busy, so they were allowed to merge. The resulting contrast of light and shade is captivating.

The formal gardens adjacent to the house lead to a circular pond which boasts a powerful jet fountain. This shoots so high that it saturates the branches of the *Rhododendron arboreum* above. With their drooping dark green foliage, rhododendrons are somewhat joyless for much of the year, but a determined effort to clean the trunks of their lower branches has revealed their contortions and the beauty of the mottled bark. Hugh and Grania extended the idea of a water garden to include a cascade, redolent of the cascade at Chatsworth, of two stepped rills flanking a flight of limestone steps above the pond. The gurgling water flashing in the dappled shade excites much comment. An Italianate feel permeates the atmosphere too: the Neptune Cascade recalls the Villa d'Este at Tivoli, near Rome.

With the ascent of the cascade completed, you notice the final formal area: a half-moon sunken garden and adjacent pergola, glimpsed across a few paces of lawn planted with flowering cherries, *Prunus* 'Tai Haku'. Designed by the Lancastrian landscape architect Thomas Mawson (1861–1933), this perennial garden is a sun trap, dug into the slope and sheltered by a south-facing wall to the rear. Shade and shelter have been thoughtfully provided by a pair of gazebos – which disappear by late summer under a profusion of climbers – from where the planting can be admired.

To the north of the sunken garden a choice of meandering paths guides you gently through the woodland gardens, where the sloping terrain and mature trees create a backdrop for more loosely structured borders. From here the tempo changes and the atmosphere becomes relaxed and informal, with specimen shrubs, trees and spring bulbs planted on grassy banks amid the canopy of trees. A long border running the length of the northern boundary wall plays host to some impressive *Magnolia* x *veitchii*, yet room has been found for the most intimate of plantings: the primrose and primula bank is as perfect a sight as anything this remarkable garden has to offer.

The long tradition of welcoming visitors to Holker Hall was encouraged when the Dukes of Devonshire owned the house: one of the duties of a housekeeper would be to show visitors the great house, whether it be the ancestral seat at Chatsworth, Hardwick Hall or Holker Hall. The desire to give visitors a warm welcome and make them feel comfortable is still uppermost in the minds of Hugh and Grania Cavendish.

In 1950 Holker Hall was one of the first houses to open its doors to visitors on a more professional basis. The present Lord Cavendish's parents were somewhat crestfallen when no one turned up on the first day, but since then it has become one of Cumbria's top visitor attractions, despite being located in the southern tip of the county, just outside the Lake District national park.

Holker Hall took a gamble when it held its first Garden Festival in 1994. This has since become a permanent fixture on the calendar in early June and is a three-day celebration of gardening, food and crafts. Nurseries in a great horticultural marquee, show gardens and demonstrations of time-honoured crafts, many unique to Cumbria, all jostle for attention. The festival has metamorphosed with the years, sometimes increasing the emphasis on food, especially with the recent

ABOVE The garden in spring.
BELOW The Neptune Cascade, beside a pink *Rhododendron arboreum*.

growing interest in food and drink, and close connections have been made with food experts such as Clarissa Dickson Wright. The countryside aspect has always been strong, with demonstrations of drystone walling and other traditional skills. Hugh and Grania make sure that every exhibitor is given a personal welcome, as they see the garden festival as a way of forging links between exhibitor and customer. The festival also helps the local economy, which depends on tourism, as thousands of visitors stay in the area.

The theme of food and drink continues with the monthly weekend markets have taken place during the summer since 2008, celebrating the best of local food producers. Purveyors of cheeses, the famous Cumberland sausage and countless other varieties, smoked fish and game, all present their products outdoors in the café courtyard.

Much thought has been devoted to extending the season. At the end of the October half-term week there is a celebration of Hallowe'en with spooky walks in the park and lantern competitions. It is not long then before the popular Christmas market enlivens November with music and braziers, crafts and food stalls. Since 2008, the success of these events has led to the house being decorated for Christmas and open to view until the festivities begin in earnest.

Schools are always welcome to visit and the education room is designed for interactive studies. These visits help children to gain an understanding of how the countryside works and become more aware of light and shade, smell and textures, water and birdsong. On-going school projects encourage repeat visits, and many children encourage their parents to return to Holker. A season-ticket scheme gives visitors the opportunity to return time and time again.

As a young couple not long married, Hugh and Grania Cavendish inherited the responsibility of Holker Hall in 1972. They also inherited a post-war debt, as many houses did at the time, in addition to the daily grind of problem-solving management in a venture that was new to them. It took fifteen years to feel that they had honed their management skills. They can now look back on almost four decades as successful custodians. Moreover, they are in the happy position of being able to hand Holker Hall and the estate on in better condition than they found it.

After almost forty years there is often a danger of becoming stale. The Cavendishes are always happy to embrace new ideas, but they also recognize that their energy levels are not as elastic as they used to be. These thoughts instigated a radical rethink about the management and future running of Holker.

They felt it was time for a new approach that would inject fresh ideas and allow scope for major delegation. Consequently a new post was created and their new chief executive arrived in 2008, with several years of running Castle Howard in Yorkshire behind him. The succeeding years have proved most fruitful. To their great relief, the time Hugh and Grania Cavendish once devoted to the everyday running of Holker has diminished considerably. They are delighted that they now have more time to be more involved with new inspirations and long-term planning. They also concede that they often have to work harder to keep abreast of innovations. As the daily problem-solving is not so dependent on them, they feel much more relaxed, and are satisfied that the required infrastructure is firmly in place. The machinery is running smoothly.

For the immediate future it is envisaged that their elder daughter, Lucy, a successful artist, will work with the chief executive and the team at Holker, as her parents gradually continue to reduce their input but hone their consultancy skills.

It is not so very long ago that the local community would look up to the vicar, doctor, school and the 'big house' for leadership; in a rapidly changing world the Cavendishes feel that this is a tradition that needs upholding. They also believe that it is important to reinvest and be seen to be reinvesting in the business that is Holker Hall. The aim is to build on the slick standard of professionalism for which Holker Hall is noted. In all respects Holker is opened as a large house on a landed estate, but at the same time it is presented as a family home.

The Garden Festival: three generations leave with their trophies (below top); visitors enjoy the jousting (below left and right); living statues survey one of Virgin's hot air balloons (opposite).

1536	Land owned originally by Cartmel Priory is bought by the Preston family.
1610	George Preston establishes his family at Holker.
1697	Death of Thomas Preston. Holker comes into the Lowther family when Preston's great grand-daughter Catherine marries William Lowther, who quickly becomes Sir William.
1756	Holker comes into the possession of the Cavendish family, having been left to Sir William Lowther's first cousin, Lord George Augustus Cavendish, 2nd son of the 3rd Duke of Devonshire.
1783–93	He engages architect John Carr of York to make elegant additions to east and north wings. The old formal Dutch gardens are swept away.
1794	Lord George's unmarried brother, Lord Frederick, succeeds and his nephew, Lord George Augustus Henry Cavendish, succeeds him, becoming Earl of Burlington in 1831.
1818	The front of house is faced with Roman cement.
1834	The 1st Earl's grandson, the 2nd Earl of Burlington, later 7th Duke of Devonshire, succeeds.
1838–42	The 7th Duke refaces and alters the entire house in gothic style, using architect George Webster of Kendal.
1863	A new stable block is built.
1871	The west wing, including much of the contents, is destroyed by fire.
1874	Paley & Austin of Lancaster complete the new sandstone west wing in the Elizabethan style.
1908	On the death of the 8th Duke of Devonshire, Holker Hall is left to his second son, Lord Richard.
1946	His son, Richard Cavendish, inherits.
1972	His son, Hugh Cavendish, inherits.

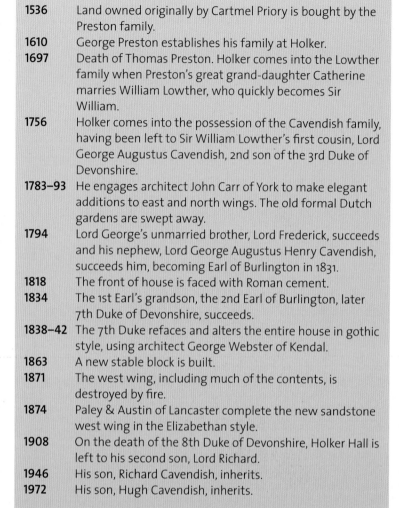

BLACKWELL

'A miracle of rare device'

The Arts and Crafts house known as Blackwell, near Bowness-on-Windermere, was built between 1898 and 1900 as a spacious, light-filled holiday home for the Holt family, who owned Holt's brewery in Manchester. They used it predominantly in the five months of summer, when it was thought prudent to avoid the risk of disease in a crowded city such as Manchester. It was designed by Mackay Hugh Baillie Scott (1865–1945), in the era of Charles Voysey and Charles Rennie Mackintosh and the period of Art Nouveau, and is the only house designed by Baillie Scott that is open to the public. Built by local craftsmen who carved the woodwork to Baillie Scott's designs of flower, leaf and berry, the house is a hymn to nature.

The changes to society forced by the First World War were unimaginable at the time of building, and after the death of the Holts' eldest son, Joseph, during the war, Blackwell became something of an anachronism. Fortunately the house was pressed into service as a school for girls from the Second World War until the mid-1970s. The school's tenancy ensured there was little change or damage, sparing it the alterations that often appear with conversion into flats or hotel, and Blackwell has emerged as the finest surviving example of Baillie Scott's work. It has been owned and immaculately restored by the Lakeland Arts Trust since 1999.

Blackwell's exterior is never bland. Limewashed walls, multiple gables and sharply graded Westmorland slate roofs evoke Lakeland farmhouse architecture of the sixteenth and seventeenth centuries (such as that of Townend, page 56), and are repeated throughout the composition. Heavyweight cylindrical chimneys and traditional sandstone mullioned windows complete the look. The beauty of limewash is that it can be applied easily as required, but after more than a century the sandstone is showing signs of erosion; Windermere has an annual rainfall

Blackwell: the north front. The house re-invents the Lake District vernacular style.

of roughly 183 centimetres/72 inches. The irregularity of gable, roof line and window and the round chimneys create a pleasingly asymmetrical restlessness. Baillie Scott enlivened the austere finish with details from the natural world, such as the plant and bird motifs on the rainwater hoppers. He also peppered the exterior with a handful of small windows, often on a different plane from that of the main windows. These reflect the preponderance of inglenook fireplaces within, with small windows often flanking the chimneypiece.

Some of the mansions around Windermere are opulent villas in the Italian or gothic style, and although we can admire them as lavish examples of their age, they could never be described as having been inspired by Lakeland farmhouses. Traditional farmhouses were normally built in sheltered locations with a south-facing aspect to maximize the warmth generated by the sun; before the days of central heating, comfort was more of a priority than the view. Blackwell, however, is perched on a wooded bluff and stands three storeys tall, commanding the fine view westwards of Windermere below and the Coniston fells beyond. Although this makes the house conspicuous, the vernacular style of architecture helps to integrate it into its surroundings.

To mitigate the exposed location, Baillie Scott located the house on a west–east axis so that he could position the main hall, dining room and drawing room on the long south side to maximize the benefit of the sun's brightness and warmth. This also creates broad contrasts inside when the oak panelling glistens on bright sunny days.

Baillie Scott sought inspiration in the medieval to create a comfortable and contemporary main hall steeped in the past. The room is reached via sliding doors from the entrance corridor and leads to the dining room beyond through a single-hinged door. Both rooms face south and the play of light on the oak panelling spangles both rooms with a warm glow. The commanding baronial feel is nowhere more apparent than in this half-timbered double-storey main hall. Baillie Scott's eye for detail builds up this manorial atmosphere. The high stained-glass windows on the south wall remind us of the days when tapestries were hung below tall windows.

The theme of home and earth is everywhere apparent at Blackwell, with honey-coloured oak panelling, green slate and pink sandstone inglenook fireplaces. It was the fireplace, and not the view, that was the prime consideration for Baillie Scott. As he explained, 'In the house the fire is a substitute for the sun. The cheerfulness we experience from the fire is akin to the delight sunlight brings.' The hearth, therefore, is the focal point in hall, dining room, drawing room and bed chamber.

As is fitting and practical for the largest room, the treatment of the hearth in the hall is bold. The lavish inglenook fireplace, with its overscaled baronial mantle, creates the effect of a miniature room within the double-storey spaciousness of the hall itself. This inglenook is made even cosier by a canopy, which seems to support the tiny minstrels' gallery above. This enclosed space has a small window and provides an elevated vantage point from which to appreciate the generous dimensions of the hall. The 'Peacock Frieze' in the hall, supplied by the wallpaper manufacturers Shand Kydd, is as old as the house, and has been restored and conserved. The panelling is a fine example of some early recycling, having come from St Mary's Church, Warwick, of 1792.

As Blackwell was designed as a holiday home with an emphasis on enjoyment and leisure, a billiard table used to take up a purpose-built area at one end of the hall, rather than being installed in its own room. Giving the table such prominence highlighted the more virile aspects

ABOVE The Peacock Frieze in the main hall, by Shand Kydd.
BELOW The hall's rowan berry frieze spills on to the doors.
RIGHT ABOVE The corner of the hall was designed to incorporate a billiard table.
RIGHT BELOW A hessian wall covering above the half-panelling dominates the dining room.

of leisure, which helps to reinforce the already strong masculine feel to this room, with its bench seat no doubt used by spectators and players enjoying a fine cigar. The half-dozen dish-shaped copper-shaded lights are original and were discovered, safely tucked away in a cupboard, by the Lakeland Arts Trust.

The far end of the main hall leads seamlessly into the dining room and it is easy to imagine the flow of Edwardian house guests gliding elegantly from one room to the other. Baillie Scott unified the two rooms with limestone quarried in Ancaster (near Grantham in Lincolnshire), Broughton slate and Delft tiles in both fireplaces. The fireback here is early Georgian, with the date 'GR 1723'. Pew-like seats and a generous sweeping arch frame the inglenook and light pours in through small stained-glass windows on either side and the room's main south-facing one.

The room is a cocoon of half-panelling and floorboards, including the ceiling, and the polished oak atmosphere is predominantly masculine. However, the rare block-printed hessian wall covering dominates the room, in the same way as the patterned leather at Levens Hall and Muncaster Castle. The hessian overflows with nature's bounty; stylized foliage and flowers twine together against a blue background faded to brown. Spring and autumn collide with small birds pecking at bluebells among a carpet of daisies, while larger birds hide among weeping rowan branches weighed down with clusters of berries.

It is impossible to underestimate the thrill of the contrast between the masculine atmosphere that prevails and the white drawing room. The drawing room makes the most theatrical impact in the house and could hardly be more different from the main hall. Baillie Scott heightened the sense of drama by placing it at the end of a long hallway that runs parallel to the north elevation, gradually becoming lighter as the size of the windows increases. Towards its furthest extremity the hallway broadens and white-painted oak panelling spills out from the drawing room, acting as a prelude to the delights within. His placing of the drawing room's west-facing bay window (which has the best view in the house) opposite the double entrance doors further heightens the theatricality and makes it the climax of the main corridor. Seeing dramatic view of sunsets over the lake and the Coniston fells from the window seat must be one of the finest sedentary experiences in the Lake District.

The white drawing room is so described because the panelling, the frieze above and the delicate ceiling plasterwork are all in white. It is the lightest room in the house, being south-west facing, with a double aspect and therefore bright and cheerful even on cloudy Lakeland days. On sunny days the large south-facing window allows all the available light to leap across the room. As the prevailing winds are westerly Baillie Scott avoided making the room draughty with a large picture window to the west. Instead he placed a modestly proportioned bay window on the western elevation; this frames the view without introducing a large expanse of glass.

The inglenook fireplace is delicately handled, with elegant iron shafts opening into leaf capitals, and it is illuminated by a small stained-glass window and

The white drawing room. By placing the main reception rooms on the south side of the house, Baillie Scott ensured they were filled with light.

The Arts and Crafts Bedroom.

slivers of mirror. A display cupboard with glass doors above the fireplace echoes the glazed double doors into the room.

Simon Jenkins calls this 'one of the loveliest twentieth-century rooms in England'. The neutral white background acts as a superb foil, so that the full impact of sky, water and the greens and greys of the fells is thrown into relief. For all its neutrality, though, white is an emotive colour. Vita Sackville-West's White Garden at Sissinghurst Castle in Kent, for instance, has excited the popular imagination the world over. Although Blackwell is a Victorian building dating from the end of the nineteenth century, Baillie Scott's use of white was perhaps saluting the dawn of a new century, in which the interior decorator Syrie Maugham would reject dark Victorian colours and popularize the notion of rooms entirely decorated in white during the 1930s.

Blackwell has nine bedrooms, three of which face east, three south and one west. Only two rooms face north. Five bedrooms are open to view: one as a bedroom, one as a history of the school and three as galleries with changing exhibitions.

Each room is has its own personality, and contains arched, plaster or panelled ceilings. When a room was originally decorated, its individual colour scheme unified the room, linking the walls with the windows and the fireplaces with the tiled surrounds.

The west-facing Arts and Crafts Bedroom, also known as the Jocelyn Morton Room, comprising a bedroom and a dressing room, has been furnished in the style of the period. As this room is above the white drawing room, the window seat affords an elevated view of Windermere. The 1920s bedroom suite is of local manufacture by Arthur W. Simpson of Kendal.

On the north elevation, Miss Murphy's Room has a display featuring the history of the house and contains photographs of Blackwell's time as a school, plus one of the original plaster ceiling moulds for the white drawing room, considered the finest ceiling in the house. In the en-suite master bedroom, now known as Gallery Two, the recurring theme of the inglenook fireplace is repeated with a miniature version of the Broughton slate and Ancaster stone fireplaces in the main hall and dining room. Although the house was originally wired for electricity and central

The south elevation, with Windermere and the Coniston fells to the west.

heating installation, a fire would have provided a warming focal point. With its generous bench seating and stained-glass windows flanking the fireplace, this room must have delayed many a proposed early start to the day. The placing of bright yellow tiles around the fireplace helps to distinguish this area almost as a room within a room. The bedroom door handles have been inspired by natural forms; replicas commissioned locally when the house was restored, they are a joy to touch.

A small copse of rhododendrons corralled by railings is a reminder that private gardens in the vicinity excel at this style of gardening. But in spite of the potential for growing rhododendrons, it was never envisaged that the garden would be extensively planted because Blackwell was to be used as a holiday home. Linking the house and garden with the views of fell and water through low-maintenance and simple plantings were key thoughts at the time, as was the pursuit of pleasure, delineated by the two lawn tennis courts.

Blackwell's elevated position almost demands terraces, aesthetically to capitalize on the panoramic view of the Coniston fells and practically to make sense of the changes in level, for the house sits on a slope. In the same way that its interiors are spacious, the generous terraces seem intended as outdoor rooms from which to enjoy the view. The high retaining walls made of slate are tailor-made for clematis and other climbers.

Contemporary plantings sit well with the timeless architecture of the house. The rowan leaf and berry decoration that gives the interior so much rhythm and repetition flows into the garden with groupings of several rowan trees.

Each year Blackwell welcomes around 40,000 visitors, who come to be inspired by its beauty and the tranquil environment, and these positives are built upon with quality lectures and exhibitions. The philosophy is to make the house look lived in and not like a static museum, so several loans of key Arts and Crafts pieces have helped to beef up the interiors.

The Lakeland Arts Trust has found that most visitors (60 per cent) come from outside the county, and either come via word of mouth or are making a repeat visit. Many of those who come more than once a year will tour the house only once; almost 20 per cent more visitors pop into the contemporary crafts and book shop and the tea room than take another look around the house. More than ever before, visitors seek out anything new, whether it is an additional piece of furniture or an exhibition. Only during the ten days it normally takes for exhibitions to be changed do numbers reduce slightly. The Trust feels that it cannot afford to become complacent about visitor numbers and works hard to encourage a sense of loyalty. Its thriving Friends of Blackwell group numbers 1,500 supporters, over half of whom receive a weekly email; a few take the trouble to reply and so a dialogue begins to form.

Blackwell also has to rise above being regarded as Windermere's 'main attraction for a wet day'! By increasing the number of photographs showing parasols and bright blue skies in its promotional literature, the trust hopes that visitors will engage with the idea that Blackwell is very much an outdoor place too, although lunch on a peaceful terrace overlooking Windermere should hardly need promoting.

The main hall is kept deliberately uncluttered, to ease its transformation into an auditorium for evening lectures. Regular free events are open to all. You can meet the curator in the main hall every Monday afternoon to discuss aspects of the house and the Arts and Crafts movement. Any group of fifteen or more can enjoy an introductory talk, adapted to their particular interest as required. Art college visits of around twenty are always welcome. The Margaret Lawler study room has Arts and Crafts books available. Sculpture and art installations in both the garden and house are becoming increasingly popular.

Activities in the shoulder months help spread the amount of business more evenly throughout the year. In spring Mother's Day has always been a big event, and in recent years Hallowe'en is galloping hot on its tail in second place, helping to make a good finish to the main season before the clocks change.

After a decade of opening Blackwell to visitors since 2001, the Lakeland Arts Trust looks forward to hosting further changing exhibitions, which inject new life throughout the year, and to loaning items that will help to create the atmosphere of the day. Blackwell was largely unfurnished when the trust first opened the house and the furniture presently on display has been purchased, lent or bequeathed. The trust will continue to seek out Arts and Crafts furniture, fixtures and fittings and is ever grateful to receive bequests.

The buoyant interest in the Arts and Crafts movement continues to keep prices high for quality items coming up for sale. Just one of the wooden blocks from which the ceiling moulds in the white drawing room were taken was recently purchased for £8,000, and a good William de Morgan fireplace tile can fetch £2,000. Even though the prices are daunting, the continuing enthusiasm for the Arts and Crafts movement is encouraging news for Blackwell.

1889	Sale of Storr's Hall estate.
1898	Sir Edward Holt, a brewery owner from Manchester, commissions Blackwell.
1900	Blackwell completed.
1915	Sir Edward Holt's eldest son killed at Gallipoli.
1928	Sir Edward Holt dies and leaves Blackwell to his second son, Edward. Edward Holt rents out Blackwell.
1942	Huyton School for Girls evacuated to Blackwell from Liverpool.
1945	Huyton School for Girls returns to Liverpool and Blackwell School is formed.
1968	Edward Holt dies.
1972	Blackwell School closes.
1972–6	Blackwell goes into private ownership.
1978	Blackwell changes hands and is used as a gymnasium, then offices for English Nature.
1999	Lakeland Arts Trust purchases Blackwell.
2001	25 September opened to the public by HRH the Prince of Wales.

ABOVE Detail of the rowan berry frieze in the white drawing room. BELOW 'Daisy' tile by William de Morgan, *c.*1890, in a bedroom fireplace.

WRITERS'
HOUSES

WORDSWORTH HOUSE

'He on honey-dew hath fed'

Wordsworth House in the west Cumbrian town of Cockermouth is famous for being the poet Wordsworth's birthplace and family home until he was thirteen. In addition to having this famous connection, the house is a rare example of a Georgian townhouse, in the care of the National Trust since 1938.

During the first decades of the eighteenth century the house was a tied property, occupied by various landowners' agents as a perk of the job. The Wordsworth family makes its first appearance in 1764, when the twenty-three-year-old John Wordsworth became agent of Sir James Lowther, later the 1st Earl of Lonsdale, with the then substantial salary of £100 per annum. Lowther was one of the most influential and wealthiest men in England, having inherited a fortune, enormous estates and the Whitehaven collieries at the age of fourteen. Wordsworth House was the Wordsworth family's home for almost twenty years until 1783 and John's son William spent his formative years here.

When William was thirteen, the death of his mother aged thirty in 1778, followed by that of his father five years later, precipitated the departure of the five children, who were accommodated elsewhere. William and his brother Richard attended Hawkshead Grammar School, and his sister Dorothy was found a new home with relatives in Halifax. Hitherto, the young William had enjoyed a happy childhood, inheriting a love of literature from his father as well as forging a close bond with his sister Dorothy. Moreover, he was inspired by the Lakeland landscape.

The house continued to be lived in by lawyers representing the Lowthers' interests until well into the nineteenth century. Fortunately, when the house was eventually sold in 1885, it was bought by Robinson Mitchell, who only made a few minor improvements to the house and garden. His ownership was followed by that of three successive doctors, who used the house as a combined home and surgery for thirty years from 1907.

PREVIOUS PAGES Wordsworth's library at Rydal Mount.
LEFT Wordsworth House dominates Cockermouth's main street.

The house's darkest hour came in 1937, when Cumberland Motor Services planned to demolish it to build a new bus station. The hammerblow of demolition was triumphantly evaded when the townsfolk formed the Wordsworth Memorial Fund, purchased the house and handed it to the National Trust. Wordsworth House enjoyed a major restoration in 2003–4 and its unique qualities are presented as hands-on interactive living history.

The imposing house dominates the main street, with its two storeys standing high above the basement level, presently limewashed in a glorious apricot. Although the house was built in 1690 by William Bird, it has a Georgian overlay of a Doric porch and sash windows, and contains decorative plasterwork and woodwork of the period within. These improvements were carried out by the Sheriff of Cumberland, Joshua Lucock, in 1745, as indicated by the inscription over the back door.

To enter, you ascend the wide steps to the Doric porch. This would have been the entrance for tenants and clients attending an interview with John Wordsworth. Inside, the fluted Corinthian columns framing the magnificent staircase give you the measure of the place. The hall leads to the front office, where John Wordsworth would have conducted his business transactions. The mahogany desk is one of the few original family pieces and is on loan from the Wordsworth Trust; it is dated 1766, the year of John Wordsworth's marriage to Ann Cookson. The National Trust reflects the fact that prints were fashionable in the eighteenth century by displaying a collection of maps, prints and portrait engravings.

The spacious and elegant dining room is appropriate for Sir James Lowther's up-and-coming agent and lawyer. It is believed that John Wordsworth added the carved overmantels here and in the drawing room during the years he was in residence.

Elevated above the street and the basement, the dining room is on the ground floor in the manner of a piano nobile (the main storey of a building, elevated above the stench of the street below, as in Palladian architecture). Paint samples from the elaborate plasterwork ceiling (the only one in the house), cornice and woodwork confirm the room as being decorated in this style in 1744–6. Its richness indicates that it was used for family dining on special occasions and for entertaining. The room was replastered in the nineteenth century so the original eighteenth-century colour has been extinguished, but the National Trust makes a convincing case for the mid-green emulsion above the dado wainscot, now marketed as 'Breakfast Room Green' by Farrow & Ball. The woodwork painted in a flat oil lead white suggests a crispness in keeping with the spirit of the age.

The Georgian simplicity is emphasized by the absence of curtains, commonly believed at the time to retain an odour of food. The dining table and sideboard were presented by the twentieth-century conductor Sir Adrian Boult. As middle-class Georgians Wordsworth's parents would have wanted the latest

RIGHT The dining room, the only room with a decorated plasterwork ceiling.
FAR RIGHT, ABOVE The entrance hall, used only for important visitors.
FAR RIGHT, BELOW The front office, which John Wordsworth used as Sir James Lowther's land agent and for his private legal practice.

ABOVE The drawing room, which the Wordsworths used for entertaining.
RIGHT ABOVE The kitchen, with a roasting spit in front of the fire and to its right the 'beehive' oven for baking bread and cakes.
RIGHT BELOW The fireplace in the common parlour, where the Wordsworth family spent most of their time indoors.

style in furniture and the Hepplewhite mahogany dining chairs, although not original to the house, are a reminder of the sudden availability of mahogany in the eighteenth century, shipped back as ballast on empty vessels.

The elegant drawing room is located on the first floor. The Corinthian-headed pilasters flanking the fireplace and the broken pediment over the door were executed with a flourish and it is thought that Joshua Lucock added the decorative woodwork and plasterwork in the early 1740s. The National Trust has returned the panelling to the soothing olive green that paint samples indicate were the original colour. The skirting is chocolate brown. In addition to their associations with the Wordsworth family, the furnishings offer an excellent insight into late Georgian middle-class pretensions. The link with the family is indicated by Wordsworth's bureau bookcase of *c*.1780, given by the poet's great-granddaughter, and the early eighteenth-century walnut chairs with horsehair seats, which were in the possession of the poet Robert Southey, a friend of Wordsworth's, who settled in Keswick. The furniture has been arranged for intimate social groups, as if the ladies are about to withdraw from the dining room after dinner, while the men continue to drink wine, before joining them later for dancing or card-playing.

The room is enlivened by the playing of a walnut-cased harpsichord. This is a replica, modelled on one that is thought to have belonged to the composer George Frederick Handel. After the death of John Wordsworth, items sold included a large and handsome Wilton carpet, which

is thought to have been in the drawing room. The new Wilton carpet was woven to a design inspired by the rug in the children's bedroom at Townend.

It was quite usual for husband and wife to have separate rooms in the eighteenth century. Wordsworth's parents each had their own bedrooms, joined by a connecting doorway, located on the first floor of the south front overlooking the street. In Ann Wordsworth's bedroom the National Trust has created a restful feminine atmosphere using a pretty white linen lawn with a green sprig pattern, which dresses a Chippendale-style four-poster bed and festoon curtains. It is a copy of an English fabric from 1765 and is lined with pea-green vegetable-dyed linen. The panelling is painted in flat oil pale grey, with oil eggshell chocolate skirting. The adjoining closet, used as a dressing room, has had similar treatment with a replica of a 1760s paper and border. The lady of the house would have expected to vacate her room when important guests such as Sir James Lowther came to stay.

The bedroom immediately behind these, overlooking the rear garden, is thought to have been the children's room; all five may have occupied it. It would have been furnished with slightly old-fashioned furniture handed down from their parents. The replicas of toys here are made from wood or cloth, a far cry from today's distractions.

The common parlour was a multi-purpose family room, used for informal everyday dining, and it would have been a convenient place for Ann Wordsworth to work in while knowing exactly what was going on in her kitchen.

The kitchen transports us straight back to the eighteenth century and is full of reminders and smells of the time when rich spices and rum were being newly imported via the busy port of nearby Whitehaven. Food was roasted, boiled or stewed on the cast-iron range that dominates the room. The roasting spit was turned by a smoke-jack fitted to the chimney breast, powered by the rising hot air. A boiling copper can be seen to the right and the charcoal stewing stove on the left was used for making sauces.

Visitors can learn about the traffic of spices into the west coast ports as volunteers in Georgian costume serve tempting samples of Cumbrian delicacies such as Cumberland rum butter made from soft brown sugar, butter, spices and dark rum. The replica sycamore table would have been the equivalent of the present-day work top and in constant use.

Wordsworth became a keen designer and gardener in later life and his first memories would have been of his parents' garden at his childhood home.

The National Trust has created a replica of a 1690s walled townhouse garden unique to the county. Bordering the river Derwent, the rear garden has its original structure of a fruit and vegetable garden, in the style of the period that the Wordsworths may well have adopted. This level rectangular plot,is typical of many town gardens. A change of level is introduced by a raised terrace running along the far wall and backing on to the river below. This terrace offered a view of the river, a place for exercise and a playground for the children, which William recalled in *The Prelude*. Although the garden would have been open in the family's day, birch, lime and copper beech planted in the early 1900s offered shade and privacy. Regrettably the trees had to be felled after 19 November 2009, when water levels in Cockermouth rose to 2.5 metres/8 feet 2 inches, and the basement level of the house and gardens were flooded (an event recalled in an exhibition in the basement). The terrace had to be rebuilt from scratch and the garden was replanted in the autumn of 2010.

A second, smaller walled garden to the east of the large one, which also contains fruit trees and other plants, has a small plat, or lawned area, and contains a replica Georgian hen house complete with hens.

In the Wordsworth family's day only the gardens of the aristocracy enjoyed the luxury of ornamental flowers. For a middle-class family the garden was a hard-working area for growing fruit and vegetables. Bearing this in mind, when the National Trust eradicated the central lawn in 2004 it returned the garden to an ordered arrangement of beds divided by narrow grass or gravel paths in the style of an allotment. This layout reflects the fact that plants were grown to be easily accessible for picking and cropping and gives a good insight into how a hard-working kitchen garden functioned in those days.

Wherever possible, only plants that the Wordsworths would have recognized in the late eighteenth century have been chosen. The walls are taken full advantage of with espaliered apple and pear trees (trained horizontally on wires) and in the beds tall perennials such as angelica and *Verbena bonariensis* lend height. Plants were not only grown for food, of course: physic beds were a necessity, used to supply fresh plants for medicinal purposes. Medicinal herbs such as bistort, tansy, self-heal, hedge woundwort, feverfew, red valerian and hyssop can be found on the wall borders running the length of the garden.

1690s	William Bird is the first owner.
1744	The first changes made by Joshua Lucock, Sheriff of Cumberland, who purchases house for £350 and adds the classical-style decorative woodwork, plasterwork, sash windows and impressive porch.
1760s	Sir James Lowther buys the house.
1764	As Sir James's agent for his Cumberland estates, a young lawyer named John Wordsworth moves into the tied house.
1766	Marriage of John and Ann Wordsworth.
1768–74	Births of their five children, including William in 1770.
1778	Death of William's mother, Ann.
1780	John updates the fireplaces with carved overmantels.
1783	Death of William's father, John; the children have to find new homes.
19THC	Still in the ownership of the Lowther family, the house is lived in by their lawyers. Few changes are made.
1885	Auctioneer Robinson Mitchell buys the house and makes pleasing improvements to the house and garden.
1907–37	The house is used by three successive doctors as a surgery and home.
1937	The house is sold to Cumberland Motor Services, who plan to demolish it. Anxious local residents form the Wordsworth Memorial Fund and raise £1,625 to buy it back.
1938	The house is donated to the National Trust and first opens to the public on 3 June 1939.
2004	The house and garden are restored to appear as they might have looked in Wordsworth's day.
2009	When the river Derwent bursts its banks on 19 November the whole of Cockermouth is flooded but only the cellars and the garden of the house are affected.

The National Trust is keen to promote Wordsworth House in Cockermouth as a hands-on Georgian experience, an interactive living history accessible to all. The sight of costumed servants immediately transports the visitor back to the late eighteenth century, but it is perhaps in the living and working kitchen, where tasters from eighteenth-century recipes are presented, that the eighteenth-century displays come into their own.

During the summer school holidays the house has to compete with all the attractions of central Lakeland. In order to encourage families, the trust stages a different daily event such as making pomanders, decorating plant pots, making pastry fish, offering children's trails in the house and garden or listening to Cumbrian ghost stories by the kitchen fire. The plight of young William becoming an orphan at the age of thirteen and having to leave his home should strike a chord with today's young visitors, and the trust is keen to target accompanied children of primary school age.

The unusual sound of the harpsichord being played by volunteers filtering through the house from the drawing room is an instant reminder of pre-gramophone and wireless days. All these activities help cut through the hi-tech times we now take for granted and keep time-honoured interests alive for new generations. You can also experience writing with a quill pen and ink. Poetry readings, talks and garden tours are all permanent fixtures in a busy calendar. Special events, such as the re-creation of Election Day in 1744, see all house staff dressed in period costume.

The rear garden was used for growing fruit, vegetables and plants with medicinal uses.

DOVE COTTAGE

'Deep romantic chasm'

A fter a four-day journey on 20 December 1799 from Sockburn-on-Tees via Yorkshire and Westmorland William and his sister Dorothy Wordsworth arrived at Dove Cottage in Grasmere. Wordsworth was twenty-nine and Dorothy would be twenty-eight on Christmas Day. In those days it was known as Town End Cottage and could be found on the old road between Ambleside and Keswick via Dunmail Raise.

From his days at Hawkshead Grammar School Wordsworth had retained fond memories of Grasmere. He captured his initial thoughts in 'Home at Grasmere':

> Once on the brow of yonder Hill I stopped . . .
> And, with a sudden influx overcome
> At sight of this seclusion, I forgot
> My haste, for hasty had my footsteps been.

After spending the winter of 1798–9 in Germany, Wordsworth had discovered Dove Cottage by chance after he returned to Lakeland. During an ambitious walking tour he had decided to return to the vale of Grasmere and was struck by a charming cottage with a rent of £8 per year. This was not the cheapest rent for a cottage at the time, but it was within his means. He immediately recognized how suitable it would be for him and Dorothy, and was set to pursue a dream.

The setting and view were magnetic, and in many ways more appealing than the cottage itself. The white roughcast cottage is a three-up and three-down building, with a buttery over a stream where beer was kept cool and provisions stored, and over which can be found a box-room extension used as the children's room. The cottage was formerly a public house, the Dove and Olive Bough, well known as a place for travellers to find refreshment before venturing over Dunmail Raise on the route northwards from Ambleside to Keswick. Beggars

Dove Cottage from the rear garden, William Wordsworth's home during his most creative period.

and pedlars continued to call long after its original function had ceased, in the hope of receiving a few pennies or a crust; in her Grasmere journal Dorothy mentions a one-legged soldier calling for alms. It may have closed as competing pubs sprang up along the route.

From the cottage they could see two-thirds of the valley, the lake with the purple summit of Helm Crag and St Oswald's church. Wordsworth was determined 'to devote himself to literature' there and regarded his new home as a permanent residence, back in the childhood landscape he had never forgotten, where he could pursue his writing. At the age of twenty-five in 1795 Wordsworth had benefited from a legacy from his young friend Raisley Calvert, who believed in him as a poet and wanted to give him the means to write. Although Wordsworth was by no means rich, he was therefore free of the shackles of regular employment, and the interest on the capital gave him the freedom to pursue his writing. The first idyllic two years before his marriage were free of responsibility, involving daily walks, rowing and sitting in the orchard or by the lake. He and Dorothy could please themselves.

Hard though it is to understand today, Wordsworth did not become well known as a poet during the few years – less than ten – he lived in Grasmere. But the first decade of the 1800s saw him at his most fertile, composing eight and a half books of *The Prelude* here and inspired to write such famous works as 'Daffodils', 'Westminster Bridge', 'Michael' and 'The Leech Gatherer'. Here at Dove Cottage he was to know much happiness, including his marriage and the births of three of his children, although there was also turbulence: William and Dorothy had to bear the loss of their beloved brother John (who stayed with them for eight months in 1800), who drowned when his ship, the *Earl of Abergavenny,* foundered off the Dorset coast in 1805.

Today, minimal lighting and crackling fires help to create the atmosphere of a Lakeland cottage of the early 1800s. Faithfully recapturing the spirit of the young poet, it is one of the most remarkable writer's homes in the world, and the cradle of Wordsworth's most fruitful imagination. It has now become a shrine to the poet and remains one of the must-see sights in the central Lakes most of the year round. A visit in season has to be timed with care.

The first room visitors see at Dove Cottage is a parlour (as opposed to a dining room), which acts as the main domestic room. Thomas de Quincey (author of *Confessions of an Opium-Eater*) gave an illuminating description of it in *Tait's Edinburgh Magazine* of January 1839. He calls it:

> the principal room of the cottage. It was an oblong square, not above eight and a half feet high, sixteen feet long, and twelve broad; very prettily wainscotted from the floor to the ceiling with dark polished oak, slightly embellished with carving. One window there was – a perfect and unpretending cottage window, with little diamond panes, embowered, at almost every season of the year, with roses; and, in the summer and autumn, with a profusion of jessamine and other fragrant shrubs. From the exuberant luxuriance of the vegetation around it, and from the dark hue of the wainscotting, this window, though tolerably large, did not furnish a very powerful light to one entered from the open air.

Cottages would have had earth floors and plaster walls, but because the cottage had once been a public house it had dark oak panelling (to obscure smoke and spillages) and a slate floor. Pepper, the dog in the portrait here, was a gift from Sir Walter Scott to the children; he was a keen breeder of small dogs, including the Dandy Dinmont breed, and had a permanent supply of puppies to give away.

Dorothy's bedroom, tucked in behind the parlour and only separated by an oak-panelled partition, is also panelled and floored with slate. She wrote her Grasmere journal mostly here, from the middle of May 1800 until January 1803. Wordsworth took over this ground-floor room as his own, prior to his marriage to Mary Hutchinson on 4 October 1802. Dorothy went upstairs. To bring this room to life it helps to recall that on the night before William's marriage to Mary, Dorothy wore the wedding ring on her finger, and she presented it to her brother next morning before he departed just after eight o'clock. When she heard he was married, she wrote in her journal, 'I could stand it no longer and threw myself on the bed, where I lay in stillness, neither hearing or seeing any thing.' William and Dorothy enjoyed an extraordinary closeness shared by few siblings, but to keep this story in perspective it is best to remember that families were often much closer in the early 1800s than they are today.

In addition to the ground-floor parlour, the family decided that they needed another room as a sitting room for entertaining their many visitors. They had soon learned that the fire in the room used initially as Dorothy's bedroom behind the parlour smoked, so they made the most attractive room upstairs into their sitting room because the fire there drew perfectly. Moreover, this first-floor room was much lighter than the one downstairs. This decision to allocate a first-floor room as a sitting room was an unusual one at the time. In spite of its modest proportions

The parlour. Oak panelling and a slate floor elevated the cottage above the norm of plaster walls and earth floors.

of 4.5 by 3.5 metres/15 feet by 12 feet and 2.25 metres/7½ feet in height, this sitting room became the hub of the cottage. It was also devoted to writing and reading; Wordsworth also needed somewhere to write and it was to this room that he would repair after working out his compositions in the open air.

The other bedrooms were in constant use. After his marriage to Mary Hutchinson in 1802 and the births their first three children in the cottage – John in 1803, Dora, 1804, and Thomas, 1806 – the cottage was filled with 'sounds carrying easily from room to room'. As an unmarried sister Dorothy became a permanent fixture; Mary's unmarried sister Sara also lived with them. Friends visited in battalions; Coleridge, William Hazlitt, Charles Lamb, Robert Southey and Walter Scott regularly came on extended visits. When friends were in residence there might be nine people accommodated in the cottage.

The remaining two rooms were used as bedrooms, one for Dorothy and one for guests. The children's room (added on to the rear of the cottage over the buttery and extending to the roof, so never a warm room) reveals an early form of enlightened insulation, in the form of copies of *The Times* of the day, that is both practical and decorative. Dorothy described a 'small, low, unceilinged room, which I have papered with newspapers and in which we have put a small bed without curtains'. The room was redecorated in the middle of the twentieth century with genuine back copies of the paper.

In 1804 the Wordsworths created a new rear door for easier access to the back garden, which they were keen to make more use of, as it provided an escape from their cramped quarters, weather permitting. By 1808 William, as both family man and host, felt that the cottage would burst. With Wordsworth's growing family, sister and sister-in-law, and a stream of visitors, the family had outgrown Dove Cottage. They were on the move. After their departure Thomas de Quincey rented the cottage from 1809 until 1835, but was in residence for only just over a decade; he too had to depart because his family was growing. He used the cottage as a full-to-overflowing book store until the owner, Mr Benson, finally shooed him away.

Decades of tenants followed, until in 1888 the cottage was purchased by a Wordsworth disciple, Mr Lee, who wished to save it for posterity. A movement to restore Dove Cottage as the home of his most inspired years and make Grasmere a focus rather than Wordsworth's later home, Rydal Mount (see page 142), gathered momentum, successfully culminating in the purchase of the cottage by national subscription in 1890. It is now owned by the Wordsworth Trust, a charity, which relies on admissions and maintains the cottage, the Wordsworth Museum and the Jerwood Centre, which houses the library and research room.

By the time the cottage was purchased by national subscription the exterior had Victorian sash windows, which have since been replaced by smaller leaded windows. The original front door was protected by a timber porch, replaced

RIGHT ABOVE The first-floor sitting room.
RIGHT BELOW The kitchen.
FAR RIGHT ABOVE A first-floor bedroom.
FAR RIGHT BELOW Dorothy Wordsworth papered the walls of the children's bedroom with newspaper for insulation. A portrait of Samuel Taylor Coleridge can be seen through the doorway.

by a stone porch in 1939. Woodworm was rather a curse for the Wordsworth Trust in the early years and the oak floorboards in the sitting room came from Winchester Cathedral in 1927; they continue to enjoy a daily hand polish.

Whatever the weather and season, many visitors have beaten a path to the door of Dove Cottage since it opened in 1891. Such is the demand that the Wordsworth Trust only closes the cottage, museum and art gallery in January for cleaning and maintenance and still manages to host an annual weekend arts and book festival that month. Dove Cottage has both to satisfy the number of visitors who come and to make sure that the small rooms do not work against the visitor experience.

During the remaining eleven months of the year Dove Cottage never rests on its laurels. The year is filled with monthly poet-in-residence workshops, talks, and workshops for schools in which pupils are encouraged to take a creative approach to poetry writing. The Foyle Room plays host to families with children who want to try their hand at poetry writing, painting, drawing and investigating old objects. Guided walks to White Moss Common offer fine views for those seeking artistic inspiration or for those who simply love the fells. The museum and art gallery have a continuous round of changing exhibitions.

ABOVE Mrs De Quincey forgot she had left a bucket of hot coals on the landing while attending to her children.
OPPOSITE The rear garden. After the Wordsworths left, De Quincey took down their summerhouse.

1617	Mentioned as a pub, the Dove and Olive Bough.
1775	Grasmere comes to be recognized as one of England's finest landscapes, described by Thomas Gray as 'a little unsuspected paradise'.
1793	Last licence granted for the Dove and Olive.
20 DECEMBER 1799	Wordsworth moves in, aged 29, with his sister Dorothy.
1804	A new back door leading from the rear to the back garden helps them make better use of the garden. A moss-lined small hut with heather wall is built at the top of the orchard where William can muse.
1808	Wordsworth moves out and passes the cottage to Thomas de Quincy.
1809	De Quincey is granted a six-year lease on 'Town End Cottage'.
1811	De Quincey annoys the Wordsworths by hacking the garden back to let more light in for the orchard and more apples, and flattens William's garden hut.
1820	De Quincy and growing family leave for Fox Ghyll, near Rydal, and Dove Cottage becomes his book store.
1830s	The lane between Windermere to Rydal and Keswick, the main route through the Lakes outside the cottage, becomes a main road.
1835	Mr Benson, the owner, terminates De Quincey's lease and the cottage is tenanted to various people, and known as 'Dixon's Lodgings. Wordsworth's Cottage' by 1871.
1850	Wordsworth's death and burial in Grasmere begins the focus of public interest on the village where he wrote many of his greatest works. This gathers momentum throughout the second half of the nineteenth century.
1862	First proposal to acquire the cottage is broached.
1872	A letter on the idea is published.
1876	William Angus Knight looks at the cottage prior to a possible purchase.
1878	Knight publishes *The English Lake District*, which directs readers to sites of significance to Wordsworth and localizes his poems. The name Dove Cottage sticks.
1880	Knight forms the Wordsworth Society with its first meeting in Grasmere
1888	Mr Edmund Lee of Bradford purchases the cottage 'to prevent it from passing into the hands of disinterested persons'.
1889	Knight's biography of Wordsworth fixes the chronological order of the poems, rather than Wordsworth's own thematic order, in the reader's imagination, and nails his most important poems to the Dove Cottage years.
1890	Mr Lee sells the cottage and a field for £650, raised by national subscription to a group of trustees, set up by the Revd Stopford Brooke. After Shakespeare's birthplace and Milton's cottage in Chalfont St Giles, it is the third such writer's house to be held in trust.
1890s	The Victorian sash windows are replaced by smaller leaded ones as the cottage would have had originally and a wooden porch replaces the old to protect the original front door (and is in turn replaced by a stone porch in 1939).
27 APRIL 1891	The cottage opened to public at 6d. per entry by Mrs Dixon, who welcomes visitors for over thirty years until she is 94 in 1923. Her granddaughter takes over until her death in 1961.
1894	A rustic arbour created on terrace to replace William's torn-down hut.
1895	The adjacent barn is demolished.
1927	The sitting room floor is replaced by oak floorboards from Winchester Cathedral.
1950	Electric lighting is installed.
1970s	After years of fighting woodworm the decision is taken to completely restore the cottage, replacing panels and reflooring rooms.
1978	Reopening of Dove Cottage.

RYDAL MOUNT

'The milk of Paradise'

What is the key to an understanding of Lakeland if it does not include fell, water and Romantic poetry? Wordsworth's Rydal Mount is quintessential Lakeland, distilled into the home of one of England's most famous poets, and internationally revered. Rydal Mount, surrounded by fell, with flashes of Windermere and Rydal Water glimpsed through the birch and pine, is a vivid Lakeland experience where you can tread hand in glove with the poet and enjoy the little-changed steep garden which he helped to fashion out of the fellside.

After eight years of sharing Dove Cottage (see page 134) with his sister Dorothy, wife Mary, sister-in-law Sara and three children, plus countless friends staying overnight, the Wordsworths needed a larger home. With no regular income to support his family, there was no question of William having the wherewithal to buy a house, so the family moved to rented property in Grasmere. Wordsworth had described Allan Bank as an 'abomination' when it was built. Nevertheless, they left Dove Cottage in the early summer of 1808, and remained here until the summer of 1811. They departed to rent the Parsonage in Grasmere, which they soon found to be damp and where had to endure a double tragedy.

Two of their five children, Thomas, born 1806, and Catherine, born 1808, died here within six months of each other, in the second half of 1812. Even though they lived in an age of high child mortality, the effects should not be underestimated. The Wordsworths' friend de Quincey was so devastated by the three-year-old Catherine's death that he flung himself on her grave night after night for two months after her death. With the children buried in St Oswald's churchyard, memories of Grasmere became too dreadful to bear. The family was in need of a complete change and the Grasmere days came abrubtly to a close.

By the end of 1812 William Wordsworth was forty-two and, although he had carved out his reputation in less than a decade at Dove Cottage, it had become painfully obvious that poetry was not giving him a sustainable income. He was so anxious about his precarious finances that he used his deceased

Rydal Mount's gable end and round Westmorland chimney were built in the sixteenth century, while the main part of the house dates from the middle of the eighteenth century.

The dining room, in the sixteenth-century cottage end of the house.

father's former connection with the Earl of Londsdale to request a secure position and income. Before an appointment could be found however, he offered Wordsworth a pension of £100 per annum out of his own pocket. By March 1813 Wordsworth had become Distributor of Stamps for Westmorland, which involved collecting taxes on legal documents for the government. This position, guaranteed for life, along with the pension, gave him an annual income of £200. This was a fortune then: the days of milk and potatoes were over and Wordsworth was set up for life, with none of the worries of spiralling inflation that exist today.

The next step was to release themselves from the Parsonage and find a permanent, spacious and comfortable home. A substantial house in almost 2 hectares/5 acres elevated above Rydal Water and convenient for Ambleside (where his seldom-used office is still located) was available for letting. Rydal Mount fitted the bill in all respects, although Dorothy Wordsworth was keen to point out that they were not 'setting up for fine folks'. If Grasmere was the working village, the Ambleside area was several notches higher on the social scale, with its gentrified old county families and people of quality. This was the perfect setting in which Wordsworth could polish his reputation as a national treasure.

The Wordsworths came to love Rydal Mount, which was fortunate, as they had only visited but not succeeded in viewing the interior before arriving on May Day in 1813. Originally a sixteenth-century humble yeoman's cottage, the property had been extended in the eighteenth century to make an imposing house. In spite of their new-found income, they set to furnishing it with cartloads of second-hand furniture from local sales. With fine views of the northern reaches of Windermere and 1.6 hectares/4 acres of garden dropping down to Rydal Water, their new home seduced them with the seclusion they had been seeking. The grounds and the superb setting also inspired Wordsworth to develop his potential as a gardener and garden designer.

The drawing room and the library were knocked through into one room in the 1960s.

Wordsworth was to spend almost forty of his eighty years at Rydal Mount. Today its long association with the Wordsworth family has ensured that it stands as a fine example of a cultured gentleman's residence.

Arriving at Rydal Mount's front door with your back to the distant view of Windermere, you look at the gable end of the sixteenth-century cottage and its prominent cylindrical Westmorland chimney. Abutting this is the eighteenth-century house, which is set at right angles so that the front of the new house embraces this fine view. (Remember that cottages and farms were usually built with the gable end facing the most exposed elevation for protection.)

You enter Rydal Mount here, through the slate porch, covered in winter jasmine. The small stone mullioned window belonging to Dorothy's bedroom on the first floor of the east elevation, only discovered in 1979, is a tangible reminder of the cottage. The drawing room has had the addition of a bay window since Wordsworth's day. The front of the house is festooned with wisteria and *Clematis montana*.

The cosy beamed dining room on the right-hand side of the entrance hall, where you are greeted and introduced to the house, is part of the sixteenth-century cottage. Above you will find Dorothy's and daughter Dora's bedroom. The original cottage entrance used to be located in the alcove, where you can see a display of Alcock's Indian ironstone plates of 1840. Its simplicity of style and furnishing still has the power to fill the room with the aura of the family.

The flagged slate floors, Delft tiles in the fireplace, 1710 spice/salt cupboard and chair covers worked by the ladies of the house – Wordsworth's wife Mary, sister Dorothy and sister-in-law Sara – give a feeling of the Wordsworths' daily round.

The drawing room was dramatically transformed in the 1960s, when it was knocked through into the library to make a large L-shaped open-plan sitting room with library shelves along one wall. The bay window was installed after Wordsworth's death and floods the room with light. You have to imagine the library in Wordsworth's day, when a servant said, 'This is my master's library where he keeps his books; his study is out of doors.' In spite of the various changes, this room would not be unrecognizable to Wordsworth, and he still presides here in spirit: it is on record that even hard-bitten Wordsworth tutors who have taught his poetry all their lives have melted when they felt his presence here. A refreshingly unstuffy approach prevails. The absence of ropes or barriers allows visitors to sit in the poet's personal chair, the rationale being that this is not the original upholstery and anything startlingly new-looking needs the corners knocking off it. Meanwhile the splitting corners of the original antique leather settee are held together with tape.

Lord Byron may have sneered that Wordsworth made himself agreeable at dinner at Lord Lonsdale's and Browning scorned, 'Just for a handful of silver he left us, just for a riband to stick in his coat', but in this room Wordsworth was fêted. Among the good and the great who attended him was the Dowager Queen Adelaide, widow of William IV, the last king before Queen Victoria ascended the throne, who was entertained here in 1840. Wordsworth and

BELOW LEFT Wordsworth's chair in the bay window of the drawing room.
BELOW RIGHT The leather sofa in the library is the original one Wordsworth used.

Samuel Taylor Coleridge became estranged from 1810 onwards, but although Coleridge himself never visited, his children were often welcomed, and a good friendship was forged between Coleridge's son Hartley and Wordsworth. The only known portrait of Dorothy Wordsworth in existence hangs above the fireplace, and you can ponder the accuracy of de Quincey's description of her Egyptian brown face and 'wild and startling eyes'. The portrait of Wordsworth as Poet Laureate is a copy of one painted for Mary Wordsworth by Henry Inman; the original hangs in the University of Pennsylvania. The National Trust has kindly returned the bookcase from Wordsworth House in Cockermouth.

On the first floor, the three bedrooms open to view are those of William and Mary, his sister Dorothy and daughter Dora.

William and Mary's bedroom suggests little of their personalities, but a gift of a pair of etchings of Queen Victoria and Prince Albert reminds us of Wordsworth's obligation to the monarch in the last decades of his life. Wordsworth was offered the post of Poet Laureate in 1843, ten days after the death of Robert Southey, who had lived in Keswick. His immediate reaction was to turn it down, which he did, on the grounds that he had always found writing to order a struggle. But in the previous year, at the age of seventy-two, he had retired from his post as Distributor of Stamps, securing it for his son Willy and thus relinquishing £400 of his

William and Mary's bedroom in the eighteenth-century extension.

annual income. Although sales of his poetry collections were buoyant and giving him an income of around £500 per annum, he was out of pocket by a substantial sum. Fortunately the prime minister, Sir Robert Peel, had made sure that Wordsworth became a pensioner on the Civil List with an income of £300, which almost put him back on the same footing.

As one good turn deserves another Wordsworth must have felt rather beholden to Sir Robert, especially when he urged him to reconsider. Whatever misgivings the seventy-three-year-old poet may still have had, he was forced to crush them. He could hardly refuse Sir Robert's personal assurance that 'I will undertake that you shall have nothing required of you', and this time he accepted. The royal etchings may stare out encouragingly but Wordsworth remains the only Poet Laureate never to have penned a single verse.

The other two bedrooms are on the first floor of the sixteenth-century cottage, at the dining-room end of the house, which explains their modest proportions. It is impossible to consider Wordsworth without his beloved sister, only twenty months younger than him and his lifetime companion for more than half a century: their lives were inseparable and intertwined. Dorothy became an invalid in the last two decades of her life and was confined to her bedroom during her final years, outliving her brother by five years and dying in 1855, aged eighty-three.

The narrow bedroom and tiny bed belonging to Dora is tinged with melancholy. She succumbed to tuberculosis in 1847 in her early forties, when the poet was seventy-seven. Her death badly affected him for his last three years: he and Mary were inconsolable. Although Dora had been married for the last six years of her life, she was as much her father's devoted friend as a loving daughter. The Wordsworths' planting of the daffodils near by in Dora's Field has thrust immortality on their unfortunate daughter. Wordsworth himself died here on the 23 April 1850, aged just eighty, the anniversary of the day on which William Shakespeare was born and died. Wordsworth's wife, Mary, would die in 1859, aged eighty-eight.

Wordsworth's attic study enjoys a view of Windermere.

The attic study, created by Wordsworth in 1838, is perhaps the most evocative room at Rydal Mount. It remains largely unaltered, in spite of being presented as an exhibition space, and delivers an inspiring view of Wordsworth's outdoor study: the world of water and fells, with the northern reaches of Windermere glinting in the distance.

Although Wordsworth the poet was at his most fertile at Dove Cottage, there is no denying that as well as correcting much of his work at Rydal Mount – 'Daffodils' was amended here – he produced some valuable new work too. It is well known that Wordsworth often corrected his poetry by pasting fresh sheets over old work from Dove Cottage, as if he never wished it to see the light of day again. The Wordsworth student can ponder whether the new lines were a fine-tuning of the old, or whether the original inspiration was the finer version.

Wordsworth was a passionate gardener and keen garden designer; indeed, he might well have become a garden designer had he not had other preoccupations. With his enthusiasm nurtured by the feeling that he could turn his hand to anything, he produced a fine garden. The 1.82 hectares/4½ acres overlooking Rydal Water are his outdoor memorial.

Rydal Mount is not merely a picturesque name: it is a rocky slope descending to Rydal Water, and the steep garden is hewn out of this. With Rydal Water in the south, and a fine view of Windermere sparkling in the distance, the site is a gardener's dream. As might be expected from a fervent disciple of nature, Wordsworth knew he wanted a natural garden that would

The garden, framed by beech trees, descends dramatically to Rydal Water.

harmonize with the countryside; besides, the steep gradient did not lend itself to fashionable formality. The design of the garden therefore respects the lie of the land without spacious terraces and formal gardens.

In line with his beliefs that a garden should both be in tune with the landscape and maintain the exquisite views, Wordsworth created an informal garden with enticing shady paths among unusual trees and flowering shrubs. The rhododendrons, nowadays long associated with Lake District gardens, were only just beginning to be fashionable. Another of his beliefs was that a garden should have 'trees carefully planted so as not to obscure the view'. Some terracing in the eighteenth century had begun to make sense of the space and below this Wordsworth laid out the garden as a lawn bordered with flowering shrubs. Perhaps mindful of the hut at Dove Cottage, he built a summerhouse as a point of destination on the sloping terrace. The far terrace continues from here and leads to the fell.

Rydal Mount is very much a Lakeland garden, embracing as well as taming the landscape. Paths bend to the fell's contours and the various rock outcrops indicate how stony the soil is. The garden is strong on atmosphere and it is not too fanciful to imagine Wordsworth working here, especially on quiet days when the feel of a private garden is at its most intense. As with the house, this is a family garden in which little has changed, and it is a remarkable experience to tread the garden steps made with rocks and heaved into place by Wordsworth himself two hundred years ago.

Today the multi-tasking curator and the gardener balance careful tree and shrub pruning, mindful of Wordsworth's dictum on light and views. As with most gardens there is a sense of renewal: occasional storms act as the Grim Reaper on shallow-rooted trees, and there are many challenges. Although the garden has been ringed by fencing, there is a continuing threat of deer, who nip bud, flower and leaf in an infuriatingly undiscerning manner.

Because of the length of time Wordsworth lived here, Rydal Mount is in a strong position to impart a deeper understanding of Wordsworth the poet, man and gardener. As a visitor attraction it also has the advantage of being in the heart of Lakeland, with extensive grounds for walking in. Rydal Mount is as popular a place for local residents to take their family and friends when staying in the lakes as Wordsworth's other home.

Dove Cottage is an undoubted magnet for shrine gatherers as the springboard of Wordsworth's early and most famous poetry, and those on a whistlestop tour of the Lakes will have time to visit only this. Yet visitors with more time on their hands are amply rewarded by a visit to Rydal Mount and for some this is a more satisfying option. There is no question of rivalry for visitor numbers between the two attractions. Dove Cottage is one of the most popular houses and literary shrines in the Lake District; competition would be preposterous and futile. Rydal Mount has an optimum number of visitors which it can cope with and the Wordsworth family are happy with this, and do not press for an increasing annual yield. This also safeguards the quality of the visitor experience for all who come.

After an initial welcome, individual visitors receive a brief introduction to the house in the dining room, before making their own way round. Tailored tours for groups around the house, in the garden or around Rydal village include poetry readings, wine and Grasmere gingerbread, and are kept light and informal. Rydal Mount is licensed to perform civil ceremonies and hosts these events in the drawing room/library before the party leaves for a wedding breakfast in one of the local hotels. A new tea room in Dora's Schoolroom (the reception building) has encouraged visitors to stay longer and make a visit more of an outing.

Rydal Mount likes to keep a fairly low profile regarding special events: there are occasional art exhibitions and book signings, but no major flights of self-promotion. After all, like many Lake District houses open to visitors, the house and grounds have their limitations; this is no grand residence and estate. The aim is that visitors depart with a greater understanding of the poet and the feeling that they have experienced the atmosphere of a lived-in home. The operation, honed over almost twenty years by the present curators, Peter and Marion Elkington, is best described as family owned and small scale, with a mere seven staff, who have to cover almost a full year rather than a seven-month season: Rydal Mount is open seven days a week in summer, five days in winter, and although the house is closed in January the time is dedicated to refreshing and polishing.

On 1 May 2013 the house celebrates the two hundredth anniversary of the Wordsworths making their home here.

1574	The Parish Register reveals a yeoman-style cottage on this site, owned by John Keene.
MID-18THC	Owner Michael Knott turns the small farm cottage into a substantial dwelling by building on a drawing-room wing on the west elevation.
7 APRIL 1770	Birth of William Wordsworth in Cockermouth.
1803	Mr Ford North of Liverpool purchases the house for £3,500 and names it Rydal Mount.
1808	The Wordsworth family leaves Dove Cottage to rent first Allan Bank and then the Parsonage in Grasmere.
1812	Rydal Mount is sold to Lady le Fleming.
1813	Wordsworth is appointed Distributor of Stamps in Westmorland and Penrith, freeing him from financial worries.
1 MAY 1813	William and Mary Wordsworth become the new tenants at Rydal Mount, taking up residence along with Wordsworth's sister Dorothy, sister-in-law Sara Hutchinson and three surviving children, John (9), Dora (8), William (2).
1843	After the death of Southey, Wordsworth is offered the position of Poet Laureate, refuses and accepts.
1847	Death of daughter Dora; daffodils are planted in 'Dora's Field'.
23 APRIL 1850	Death of Wordsworth at Rydal Mount, and burial in Grasmere churchyard.
1855	Death of Dorothy Wordsworth at Rydal Mount.
1859	Death of Mary Wordsworth at Rydal Mount.
1859–1969	After almost a century of various tenants, the house is eventually sold.
1969	Mary Henderson (née Wordsworth), the poet's great-great-granddaughter, purchases Rydal Mount.
7 APRIL 1970	On the bicentenary of Wordsworth's birth, Rydal Mount opens to the public.
1993	Death of Mary Henderson.
23 APRIL 2000	A millennium plaque commemorates the 150th anniversary of the poet's death.
1 MAY 2013	200th anniversary of the Wordsworths' arrival.

MIREHOUSE

'Down the green hill'

Mirehouse, located on the shore of Bassenthwaite Lake, is a seventeenth-century manor house owned by the Spedding family. In its heyday it played host not only to Wordsworth but to Alfred, Lord Tennyson (1809–92), who succeeded him as Poet Laureate, and Thomas Carlyle (1795–1881), the historian and essayist, and other nineteenth-century writers. They were all frequent visitors and friends of James Spedding (1808–81), who is now chiefly remembered for being the editor of the works of Francis Bacon.

The original house has had several extensions over the years, which have considerably improved its exterior. The late Georgian north front, complete with a porch of four Tuscan columns, is relatively modest, but the whole elevation is lifted by the two later canted bay windows of 1790 at each end. The two large

RIGHT Mirehouse enjoys a glorious location by Bassenthwaite Lake at the foot of the Skiddaw massif.
FOLLOWING PAGES The Music Room, with a glimpse of the library beyond.

bays with their generous windows admit as much light as possible on a north elevation – an essential requirement for a house that sits close to brooding Skiddaw and the pikes of Grisedale and Ullock. The bays make the front of the house far more impressive than the rear. Ranks of chimneys silhouetted against the steep wooded fell of Ullock Pike are reminders of long winters in the northern lakes. The south side was demolished in 1832 to make way for a new wing by Joseph Cantwell of London, with higher ceilings making more spacious rooms.

The west-facing single-storey wing, containing a music room and a little drawing room, was built in 1851. Later, during the 1880s, a servants' wing and a chapel were added on the east elevation, the latter being demolished in the 1960s.

Mirehouse's new dining room of 1833, fitting seamlessly into the wing of 1790, is the house's most elaborate reception room. Although strictly of the reign of William IV, who reigned from 1830 to 1837, in between those of George IV, formerly the Prince Regent, and Queen Victoria, this light and airy room exudes an elegant Georgian atmosphere, with a touch of gothic in the niche. It was later severed in two to become a butler's sitting room and pantry, but thankfully put back as one room after the two world wars reduced the staff of between twenty-five and thirty to just two.

As well as revealing much about the owner, James Spedding, and the life of a Victorian country gentleman, the drawing room is a hymn to Alfred, Lord Tennyson. Tennyson wrote the first of his great elegies to the memory of James's younger brother, Edward, who died in 1832, 'To JS'.

'In Memoriam', another of Tennyson's great works, was also written in response to the death of a dear and valued friend. It was only a year after Edward's death that Tennyson lost his friend Arthur Hallam. Hallam was the brightest star of the Cambridge group known as the Apostles and had been engaged to Emily, the poet's sister, when he died. In 1835, the still grief-stricken Tennyson was forced to sell his Chancellor's Gold Medal for English Verse for £15 to pay for a trip to Mirehouse. Fortunately his meeting there with Edward FitzGerald (1809–83) created a new lifelong friendship. The portraits in this room are a reminder of how much these friends meant to each other and to James Spedding.

The light, airy west-facing area comprising the music room and little drawing room is delightful. The music room would have been the smart social hub of the house. Its rich red

colour scheme was inspired by the portrait of John Spedding over the fireplace. The little drawing room became the favoured haunt for ladies of the house, as their sewing boxes and china reveal, and today's visitor can enjoy looking at the Burmese and military ephemera contained here.

In the smoking room Sir Francis Bacon plays a large role. There are not only first editions and collections of his papers but also James Spedding's own fourteen-volume edition of the man, covering his life, letters and works.

In the library opportunities for indoor diversions abound. It was here that James Spedding entertained some of the leading writers of the day, among them Southey, FitzGerald, Carlyle and Thackeray. The library reveals the wide-ranging interests of the Spedding brothers with shelves dedicated to philosophy, science, the classics and of course poetry. Thomas Story Spedding (1800–70) was James's elder brother, known as Tom, who added to the volumes collected by their father.

Among the letters and manuscripts are several that shed light on many a problem had by authors, such as Carlyle struggling with his biography of Frederick the Great and having to endure 'extremely dull German books' in the process. As he embarked wearily on volume two, he noted: 'If I live to get out of this Prussian Scrape (by far the worst I ever got into) it is among my dreams to come to Mirehouse.'

If Tennyson reigns supreme in the drawing room, Wordsworth dominates the study. Manuscripts of his poems and letters, together with those of Southey and Hartley Coleridge, all beckon the visitor.

In keeping with its location, Mirehouse's garden is largely an informal country garden in style. Spruces march up the steep rise of Dodd Fell behind the house and late eighteenth-century Scots pines lend an alpine feel. Not so long ago, in the 1960s, the pines were all but obliterated by overgrown rhododendrons, which had choked the drive, but order has since been restored. At about the time when the pines were planted in 1786 the walled garden was also under construction. This was replanted in the mid-1990s to encourage honeybees.

At Mirehouse you are always conscious of the surrounding fells, which help to make the rhododendrons look appropriate for their setting. The most formal area by the house is genteel Victorian, with a sheltering rose colonnade and lawns terraced in the 1850s. Today, however, the aim behind the garden is for it to complement the stunning landscape and not to impose further formal areas on it but to build on the relaxed atmosphere and natural feel of the place.

Once the carpet of daffodils in the meadow opposite the front door has died down, the land plays host to over forty species of grasses, sedges and wildflowers until it is cut for hay in July. Weedkillers and artificial fertilizers have been banished and this area acts as something of a memorial to the 95 per cent of ancient wildflower meadows that have disappeared from Britain since 1945. Further away from the house, countless woodland walks beckon the more active visitor.

Mirehouse markets itself as a gentleman's residence with literary connections and the Fryer-Spedding family is keen to keep this tradition alive. A key event is the annual poetry competition held in conjunction with the Words by the Water Literary Festival in Keswick each March. Every year the prize-winning work and eight highly commended poems are displayed on the Mirehouse Poetry Walk on the veranda behind the house. The family has also been encouraging school groups to visit since 1981.

However, the owner, James Fryer-Spedding, accepts that the logistics of a small house and estate with limited parking in the immediate vicinity of the house – visitors must walk down the drive after they have parked vehicles in the roadside car park – means that they are unable to host large events. In addition, Mirehouse is first and foremost a family home rather than a visitor attraction. Although Mirehouse does not operate a Friends' scheme, the family welcomes back those making repeat visits, and chooses to keep admission charges low, in order to make the house accessible to as many visitors as possible.

16THC	First record of the house.
1666	Present house built by the 8th Earl of Derby.
1688	House sold to agent Roger Gregg – the only time it is sold.
1780	The walled garden is created.
1786	Scots pines are planted along the drive.
1790	Matching bays are added.
1802	The house is left to John Spedding of Armathwaite Hall.
1832	The south side is demolished, and new higher rooms are built, by Joseph Cantwell of London.
1850s	The lawns are terraced.
1851	The large west rooms are added.
1880s	A servants' wing and wooden chapel added (demolished in the 1960s).
MID-1990s	Extensive restoration to the gardens includes the creation of a honeybee garden.

The library.

POESIE NARRATIVE

BRANTWOOD

'Mid these dancing rocks'

John Ruskin described Brantwood as facing 'five acres of rock and moor and streamlet'. The rock is, of course, the bulk of the Old Man of Coniston, which Ruskin would scrutinize, enjoying its countless moods as determined by Lakeland's quickly changing weather. Whether seen against scudding white clouds and a brilliant blue sky or atmospherically suffocated by curtains of rain, the view of this fell is superb. Brantwood appears to hover above Coniston Water, enveloped by the steep wooded slopes around it.

LEFT Coniston's steam boat *Gondola* takes visitors to Brantwood.
BELOW Ruskin enjoyed watching Coniston Water and the Old Man of Coniston in their many moods from the window of the turret room he built on to the house.

John Ruskin (1819–1900), art critic and social thinker, settled permanently at Brantwood on Coniston Water in his early fifties, and it became his home for the last twenty-eight years of his life. He purchased the house for £1,500 from William James Linton, a leading wood-engraver, artist, poet and political writer of the time. Like Wordsworth, who, we recall, had not viewed the interior of Rydal Mount before moving in, Ruskin took Brantwood on trust and, ironically for a place that was to fulfil so many of his expectations, bought it sight unseen in 1871. However, he knew something of its position, as before the original cottage was built this location used to be a West station – one of the key viewpoints in the Lake District, known as stations, noted by Father Thomas West in his *Guide to the Lakes* of 1778 – so this spot had been famous for decades. When Ruskin heard that the property was for sale, the stupendous view was the great draw.

Ruskin filled his home with paintings by J.M.W. Turner and other leading artists, furniture and objets d'art, but after his death in 1900 much of his prized collection was sold (or even destroyed). Fortunately in 1932 an admirer of Ruskin, John Whitehouse, a Liberal Member of Parliament and Parliamentary Private Secretary to Lloyd George, purchased Brantwood, and he began the long haul of reinstating some of the collection. The house was opened to the public in 1934 and the Brantwood Trust was formed in 1951 by Whitehouse, who died in 1955. His successor as chairman was Lord Lloyd of Kilgerran, CBE, QC, until his death in 1991. The Lloyd family and Lancaster University created the Ruskin Foundation in 1994 and this incorporated the Brantwood Trust. It has taken a lifetime to return Brantwood to looking more how Ruskin would have known it, but with the help of many important bequests, Brantwood today is one of Lakeland's most absorbing houses.

Formerly a humble cottage of *c.*1797, the remains of which are now the entrance hall and study, the house comprised a drawing room and four ground-floor rooms added around the 1830s. To extract every ounce of artistic inspiration from the view, Ruskin perched a high turret room on one corner of the first floor within his first twelve months, an eyrie from which he could

The drawing room walls are papered with a copy of the wallpaper Ruskin designed for it.

miss nothing. This was followed by the building of a lodge for his valet in 1872 and a single-storey dining room towards the end of the decade. The outbuildings near the back door were completed about twenty years later. He also acquired 202 hectares/500 acres of moor and fell over the years, and by 1900 the house had been transformed almost beyond recognition.

Many house improvements and additions were made to accommodate his cousin, Joan Severn, her husband the artist Arthur Severn, and their five children, who came to look after Ruskin at Brantwood once he was in his sixties and remained with him; Mrs Severn had looked after Ruskin's mother in London during her final years. Another ten years saw the completion of a large artist's studio to the rear for Arthur, along with a second floor with a schoolroom and further bedrooms.

Perhaps no house could quite live up to the view, and Brantwood is the sum of its various additions over the decades. But while it may not be architecturally distinguished, the result is not unpleasing. Part cottage and part villa, it creates a pleasing focal point on the sparsely populated eastern shore of Coniston Water.

Ruskin's spacious south-facing dining room extension with its generous proportions and high ceilings comes as a surprise after a succession of smaller rooms. It is a great improvement on the former north-facing dining room off the entrance hall, which now serves as a useful gallery space, as the seven windows flood the room with light. The new dining room is a surreal clash between the cool, green scenery surrounding Coniston Water and the sensory overload of Venice. You gaze across the lake to the fells through a range of mullioned Venetian lancet windows, which give the effect of a painting brought to life, as if you are viewing Lakeland from a Venetian palazzo. These seven windows, representing the seven pillars of wisdom, have since become Brantwood's logo.

The short wall is dominated by three Ruskin family portraits: James Northcote was commissioned to paint the three-year-old Ruskin in 1822, and this large portrait is flanked

In the dining room a portrait of Ruskin as a child is flanked by ones of his mother and father.

by portraits of his mother and father. Together they illuminate much that is key to an understanding of Ruskin.

Despite Ruskin's tender years, Northcote highlights several significant details that explain a lot about the man the boy was to come. His love of hills is revealed by the presence of the 'boo hills', which he precociously insisted should be included – a love that would find fulfilment in the view from Brantwood. He also felt not only that it was imperative to have his dog included, but that it had to be thrust into an important foreground position; Ruskin was to love and own dogs all his life. The pale blue sash also has a resonance: pale blue became a symbolic colour for him and was a colour he would wear until the end of his days.

George Watson's romantic portrait of Ruskin's father, John James, of 1802, shows a striking seventeen-year-old poised to make his fortune as a sherry merchant for the House of Domecq, after moving from Edinburgh to London. John James passed on his love of poetry and art to his son; not only was he an artist himself, but he showered his son with paintings, including his first watercolours by Turner, an artist Ruskin went on to champion for the rest of his life.

The social, moral and Calvinist side of his parents' marriage is hinted at in the 1826 portrait of his mother, Margaret, by this time middle-aged, strait-laced and sombre. It is not hard to imagine her dedicating herself to daily Bible readings for her son's benefit.

These portraits encapsulate some of the dynamics in Ruskin's life. The different personalities of his parents helped to make him the complex man he became. He was a precocious only child and a troubled soul as an adult. The struggle to reconcile the artist in himself with the social, moral and spiritual aspects of the Victorian era continued throughout his life.

Not many owners combine the skills of an interior decorator with those of an artist, as Ruskin did. He designed the original drawing room wallpaper inspired by a motif noted in a fifteenth-century painting he had seen in the National Gallery. The copy that was rehung in the drawing room in the 1980s still looks resplendent. The two pianos in the room are reminders that Ruskin used the room as a salon. Today's visitors are encouraged to play the grand piano and fill the room with music, just as Ruskin would have known it. His walnut upright Broadwood behind the door was recently returned to the house, but remains silent.

Almost two thousand works of art are in the trust's possession, the majority housed in the Ruskin Library at Lancaster University. Those exhibited at Brantwood are rotated, in a manner that would have been familiar to Ruskin, who frequently moved and rehung his pictures. Display cabinets are deliberately kept to a minimum, but the shelf cabinet in the alcove makes a perfect setting for objects from the collection. The terrible loss of the contents has been diluted over the years. Although many pieces of furniture once in the house were bought locally in a sale of July 1931, there has been a steady flow of them returning as their owners or families have decided that Brantwood would be the most appropriate home for them after all. The drawing room looks well furnished once more and it is not hard to imagine the daily ritual of strawberries and cream here at 10.00 a.m. while Ruskin read aloud from his morning's writing.

The study on the ground floor was the powerhouse of Brantwood, which oversaw a daily outpouring of books, essays and a prolific amount of correspondence; Ruskin's life

The study was home to Ruskin's desk and collections (far right, below).
He was enthralled by the view from the bay window (right), in front of
which were his winter table and campaign chair (far right, above).

pivots on this room. Adjacent to the drawing room, it was originally two small rooms, made into one probably by a previous owner, Anne Copley, in the 1830s. Ruskin would sit at the 'winter table' in the small bow window during the winter, always conscious of the changing weather as he did so. He was an inveterate European traveller and his collapsing campaign chair, which he used for travelling, is squeezed close to this window. It is a beautiful and evocative piece of furniture and a last vestige of the days of travelling by carriage.

Many of the portraits and photographs show Ruskin seated in this beloved chair and perhaps of all the possessions this is the piece most readily associated with him. Not only is it perched by the fireplace, the view and his books: it is directly opposite the square Turner cabinet, which housed and made the artist's watercolours accessible and easily rotated. With Ruskin's collections and books, the room epitomizes the Victorian gentleman's study. It was also a treasure trove: as well as the Turner watercolours, medieval manuscripts and those of Ruskin's own books were all contained here.

The turret bedroom must have one of the finest views of any bedroom in England. This was Ruskin's bedroom for his first six years here until illness and unsettling dreams forced him into the room adjacent, where he surrounded himself with twenty favourite Turner watercolours.

The garden sits on a rocky wooded hillside. Eight individual gardens explore themes that fascinated Ruskin as an artist and social reformer. A collection of British native ferns can be seen at their best, in damp woodland with trickling waterfalls.

At the less than tender age of fifty-two this was Ruskin's first opportunity to garden. He had always enjoyed discovering plants in his parents' London garden, but as it was not thought to be the done thing to encourage a young gentleman to garden, he had had no practical experience. Ruskin was always a multi-tasker, both in his work and the garden. Gardening was as much about experimentation as anything else for him, and he was forever pouring his energies into new projects. This often meant that last year's new experiment would screech to an abrupt standstill, but to be fair, Ruskin was still lecturing and travelling extensively, and was never able to dedicate as much of his energy as he might have liked to gardening. Several of these ventures, commenced in a blaze of enthusiasm when he arrived in the 1870s, were freeze-framed for over a century until the late 1980s.

When Ruskin first arrived at Brantwood, he was not only determined to overcome the neglect of the garden from the time of William James Linton, its previous owner, but also committed to a series of experimental horticultural and land management projects, not always running concurrently. The geologist within him devoted so much time to creating a small stone harbour that he was forced to delegate its completion. He went on to adopt Linton's subsistence garden, which became known as the Professor's Area. In this lowly mountain crofter's kitchen garden Ruskin was searching how to feed man with plants good for both body and soul while arranging them aesthetically.

LEFT Ruskin's bedroom, looking through to his turret extension.
ABOVE The turret window.

Only two thumbnail designs for Ruskin's 'Zig-Zaggy' garden, carried out in the late 1870s, survive in a letter to his cousin, Joan Severn, who was to spend many years at Brantwood. Although the detail of Ruskin's original planting has vanished, the present gardening team has realized his idea of the garden as Dante's Purgatorial Mount. The levels of Purgatory as depicted in Dante's *Divine Comedy* are represented in an allegorical zig-zaggy, an arresting and thought-provoking journey through Purgatory to Paradise.

In a large level area – an early tennis court, until located elsewhere – Ruskin was creating an image of the kind of glade you find in Renaissance paintings, with the view of the Coniston fells and water defined by the thin stems of coppiced trees. Birch trees predominate, as they have formed colonies here, although oaks, a familiar tree to Botticelli, are planned to replace them.

Everything in the garden had to have a purpose for Ruskin. Water and its place in the landscape fascinated him, as it did other Victorians. The fish pond, which would have been much more open then, became an area primarily for studying fish, which was much easier to do in a small pond as opposed to a deep lake. This study led to one of the Severn boys becoming a commercial fish farmer. The theme of water at Brantwood continued to be important in all manner of ways. In the early 1880s Ruskin's greatest project was his moorland garden, featuring terraces fashioned from the natural forms of the land and two reservoirs. This was a visionary experiment in upland geography, long abandoned, the idea being to create a harmonious balance between man and nature. Once the soil had been removed down to the rock from a high-ground stretch of bog, the water could run down to one of the two reservoirs. Ruskin also experimented with hardy wheat up here, and in the damper areas cultivated cranberries. He developed a permanent cascade controlled by sluice gates from the beck opposite the front door.

Once Mrs Severn came to Brantwood, she became the ascendant star who had great input in the garden. Her vision was a balance between Ruskin's and the aesthetic, and her ideas as a society lady, eager to impress and following the fashions of the time. She helped to dress the series of paths with plants, which led to what Ruskin regarded as jewels in the landscape, such as rocks picturesquely surrounded by bluebells or wood sorrel. Azaleas, rhododendrons and Japanese maples were in vogue in the last quarter of the nineteenth century and she made sure these fashion statements became firmly entrenched at Brantwood; they continue to be very much a part of the garden to this day.

After Ruskin's death the gardens were never ignored, but there was no injection of ideas and little inspiration, and they had to tread water for many years. The succeeding decades are a history of underfunding of what came to be regarded as essentially a Lakeland rhododendron garden and not much more.

When the head gardener Sally Beamish arrived in 1988, she soon realized that Brantwood and its 101-hectare/250-acre estate held great significance. The strategy since then has had two strings to its bow. There is an ongoing restoration of the areas as worked on by Mrs Severn, sympathetic to her ideas and achievements. Second, there is the renovation of the historic structure of Ruskin's time, such as walls and fences. Moreover, the present team is picking up where Ruskin was forced to leave off, making the garden more contemporary, but following the original basic thought and philosophy for each area. Projects based on Ruskin's philosophy include planting British herbs in the kitchen garden and forming a maze comprising the collection of 250 native ferns. The ice house was built in a cave excavated by local miners.

Brant is the old Norse word for steep and mountainside gardening at Brantwood continues to present a challenge. Working on inaccessible areas up steep slopes and keeping paths open and visitors safe go with the territory. Although lack of rainfall in the Lake District is seldom a challenge, plants soon begin to struggle in the stony soil here, especially on well-drained steep terrain in unexpected long dry spells. Straightforward moisture-retentive mulching does not altogether solve the problem and the head gardener has found that they need to use a colloidal humus, which merges with the soil and does not disappear downhill in heavy rains.

Nature is all too keen to redress the balance and it is a continual challenge when renovating tired areas to achieve an equilibrium between the garden and nature. The gardeners work with native materials, which is not always the easiest route either. The economics of Brantwood as an independent registered charity dictate that staffing levels have to be tight: the man hours available equate to three full-timers, plus a valued team of enthusiastic volunteers. Like all good gardens Brantwood is not finished, and it is still in a process of recovery, continuing in a way that Ruskin would have endorsed.

The Brantwood Trust is all too aware of the difficulties of making the former home of a famous writer attractive to visitors. A plethora of glass cabinets in dry airless spaces would make Brantwood a dreary place and do little to champion John Ruskin or his home. Having built up a strong repeat business of visitors who enjoy the location, terrace and restaurant, the trust suffered a blow when its good work evaporated with the outbreak of foot and mouth disease in the spring of 2001, when movement of traffic to and within Cumbria was reduced to a minimum (in the hope of ring-fencing the disease), seriously damaging tourism. Once the county had recovered from this catastrophe, the trust decided to refresh the visitor experience.

The trust believed that it was essential for the visitor 'to engage with the real thing' and through making a visit come to respect Ruskin. Ruskin's star was in the doldrums at the time; he is not taught in schools. This is partly because he is such a difficult man to categorize, having had a wide variety of interests and been involved in many causes. As the Brantwood trustees comment, 'John Ruskin left a legacy of influence that stretches from Frank Lloyd Wright to Mahatma Gandhi. He championed many of the tenets of the welfare state, and inspired the founders of the National Health Service, the formation of Public Libraries, the National Trust and many other cornerstones of civil society in the last one hundred years. His influence reached abroad in such areas as women's education, the minimum wage, child labour, and environmental protection and has served both as a restraining influence on unbridled capitalism and a moral conscience for the nations of the world.'

The decision to show how relevant Ruskin is today has helped to give Brantwood a dual role as a museum and a place of activities. Developments include revealing more of the estate as well as making a special feature of the gardens as well as the house. Following the path begun by Ruskin, who championed the artist J.M.W. Turner throughout his life, educational courses on historical and contemporary art support today's artists. Similarly, concerts are not just about showmanship but support today's musicians and young artists. The feel of a lived-in house, where people can be entertained with music and stimulating topics over a glass of wine, has become a paramount aim. For Brantwood, culture is not about exclusivity: whatever their education, visitors are encouraged to make their own experience and find their own Ruskin.

Ruskin was a great teacher and lecturer, and recognized the need to fire the minds and imaginations of both younger children and university-level students. Brantwood hopes that it is using memorable educational ideas such as tactile learning. The Linton building (formerly home to William James Linton's printing press) has a twenty-first-century stone xylophone, reminiscent of Ruskin's and something of a phenomenon in his day: today's visitors can play it and learn something of the geology of Lakeland. Burlington and Sandside schools have adopted part of the woodland and are learning woodland skills and crafts, such as coppicing for hurdles and baskets, and to provide wood for bark peeling, which was once used to tan leather and for charcoal burning.

Although Brantwood owes much of its charm to its unique setting, its isolated location is not always on its side: it remains on the end of the tourism chain. Visitors usually make for the central Lake District first, and after filling the arterial system some will radiate outwards and make for the Coniston valley. Holiday patterns have changed dramatically from the one- or two-week holiday to three- or four-day short breaks. Consequently high-season visitor numbers have dipped slightly but the shoulder months in spring and autumn are now busier, which relieves some of the pressure in summer. On a short break if the weather is poor for more than one day there is less time to become seriously bored and break away from the immediate vicinity of one's destination. Ideally Brantwood attracts visitors staying in Ambleside who find themselves in need of a change after a few days of the central Lakes, yet it is nigh on impossible to second guess the magic formula.

Brantwood relies on a vigorous programme of events and activities. In addition to those already described, outdoor theatre performances in summer are held against one of England's finest backdrops. Guided garden walks take place between Easter and October three to four times a week, and there are gardening and horticulture classes run by the estate manager. The Severn Studio – one of several underutilized assets which the trust realized had enormous potential – has been refurbished and is now used for conferences and events. Family trails around the woodland estate help everyone to discover more about animals and their habitat. There is a thriving programme of school visits. You can shop at the bookshop in the house or at the Cumbrian craft weekend fair in November. You can participate by joining the Friends and attending meetings and trips. Opportunities to be a volunteer seem boundless, whether it be house and event stewarding, gardening, leading estate walks, research or administration.

1797	Thomas Woodville purchases 1.2 hectare/3-acre plot near Beck Leven and builds a small house with eight rooms named Brantwood Cottage. This location was known as a West station from West's *Guide to the Lakes*: visitors would have read about it and thronged to it for the view of the Old Man of Coniston. Hence Ruskin knew precisely its precise location and its view.
1823	Samuel Carrington purchases the house.
1827	Edward and Anne Copley purchase the house.
1830	Anne Copley junior inherits and enlarges the frontage with a new room at the northern end, since incorporated into drawing room; adds the 'old' dining room and kitchens to the rear, all with higher ceilings; and makes one study out of two rooms. A coach house and stables are built, the latter now part of the Lodge outbuildings.
1833	She adds 6–7 acres of woodland.
1841	She begins leasing Brantwood and in 1844 leases it to a friend, Joseph Hudson (father of the Revd Charles Hudson, founder member of the Alpine Club) and his family.
1845	Death of Anne Copley junior. Her executor fails to sell Brantwood with the Hudsons in residence.
1852	The Hudson family departs and a leading wood-engraver of the day, artist, poet and political writer William James Linton, rents the house. By early 1853 he has raised mortgage for £1,000 and bought it. Builds outbuildings on south drive in order to set up printing press for political pamphlets; he also produces several natural history publications.
1857	After the death of first wife, Linton marries Eliza Lynn, a three-volume novel writer.
1858	Brantwood is let to the poet Gerald Massey.
1864	Having moved to London and disliked it, Linton returns to live there, with family staying during summers. The Fell Enclosure Act gives the estate an apportionment of a further 6 acres, making a total of 6.5 hectares/16 acres.
1867	Linton emigrates to America, leaving furniture and summer letting to Revd G.W. Kitchin.
1871	While convalescing in Matlock, John Ruskin hears Brantwood is for sale, and although house unknown to him he recognizes its location. He agrees to pay the asking price of £1,500, sight unseen. He repairs the roof and builds a small turret room on to a bedroom on the southern corner.
SEPTEMBER 1872	Ruskin comes to live at Brantwood, bringing Arthur Severn, son of Joseph Severn, a friend of Keats, his wife Joan and their family. Brantwood becomes the Severns' second home.
1872	Ruskin builds a new lodge for valet on site of old demolished stable block, with angled windows to catch the views.
1875	Ruskin enlarges the harbour and creates a cottage garden in the woods behind the house.
1877–9	He creates a fish pond.
1878	He builds a new single-storey dining room with French windows and seven lancet windows, releasing the 'old' dining room as a library.

1881	He creates a moorland garden behind the house.
1881–2	He blasts 100 tons of white clay and builds the present coach house with stables, and a kitchen garden where the present car park stands.
1880s	He adds a second floor to provide a school room and five further bedrooms.
1885	Ruskin executes a Deed of Gift making over Brantwood to the Severns, but retains effective ownership during his lifetime.
1886	A studio is built on to the back of the house.
1890s	The estate is increased to 500 acres by Mrs Severn.
20 January 1900	Death of Ruskin. He leaves the contents to Arthur and Joan Severn.
1905	The bay window is added to the drawing room .
Early 1900s	Most of Ruskin's collection – including medieval manuscripts, most of his Turner watercolours collection, Italian sculptures and Scott manuscripts – is sold to augment the Severns' income.
1924	Death of Joan Severn. Arthur Severn spends most of his time in London, dying in 1931.
1931	At a Sotheby's sale, and a July sale on the premises, J. Howard Whitehouse, a follower of Ruskin, collects some of the lost treasures.
1932	Whitehouse manages to buy four out of eight lots of Brantwood, including the house, outbuildings and 250 acres of land, for £7,000.
21 April 1934	Brantwood is opened to the public.
1944	Brantwood is transferred to Oxford University to ensure its future as a Ruskin memorial.
1947	For several reasons the university is forced to surrender the gift. The Brantwood Trust is established by Whitehouse as a registered charity to look after and manage Brantwood for posterity, in whose ownership it remains.
1955	Upon Whitehouse's death, Brantwood comes under the care of his successor in the trust, Lord Lloyd of Kilgerran.
1973	The Nature Trail is opened.
1982	Mains water is installed; the Linton building is renovated.
1989	National Art Collections Fund Award.
1991	Lord Lloyd dies; he is succeeded as Chairman of Education Trust by his daughter, Elizabeth Robins, and as Chairman of the Brantwood Management Trust by Michael Prince.
1992	The Ruskin Foundation is formed, with Princess Alexandra as Patron and Sir Richard Parsons as Chairman; Tony Cann, CBE, becomes Chairman of Brantwood Management Trust.
1995	Visit to Brantwood by Princess Alexandra.
1997	The Ruskin Library at Lancaster University is completed. The Ruskin Foundation takes responsibility for the entire Whitehouse Collection, to be housed jointly at Brantwood and Lancaster.
2006	Lady Lloyd dies.

You could also get married here with a civil ceremony in the drawing room or the Severn Studio. The Eyrie, which as its name suggests has an amazing view, provides self-catering accommodation within the building.

Inevitably a house such as Brantwood, transformed and extended under wealthy ownership, often suffers from underinvestment in the years that follow, and this became Brantwood's fate in the early 1900s. The trust's policy is to make ongoing improvements whenever it has to carry out routine repairs and replacements, so as to create a benefit. Whenever maintenance is required it makes sense to make as many gains as possible: this is a vital aspect of looking after a property.

A big challenge is the continually leaking chimneys: as reports conflict, no conclusion has been reached and they continue to exercise the minds of the trust and its team. In addition, Ruskin's small harbour was exposed to the flooding and high water of late November 2009, and continues to be a problem. Since the line of the shore was originally altered to accommodate it, the shingle has piled up to make an enormous bank that is hard to shift. Consequently the harbour will continue to suffer from shingle or water damage.

Self-sufficiency has to be key: a place like Brantwood needs to have a versatile all-rounder who can tackle most things, and this it has in the estate team, who are responsible for tackling as many tasks themselves as they can, such as working the timber from the estate's oaks to create fencing, compost bins and other essential objects. Not only is their work cheaper than that carried out by imported contractors, but Brantwood has more overall control. It can, though, also call on a tame network of contractors who are sympathetic to the style to which the trust is working.

Brantwood's economics are reliant on visitor numbers and the new scheme to benefit from Gift Aid should increase revenue; courses running to capacity also help enormously. No matter how successful the planning and marketing, a visitor attraction is always at the mercy of outside upheavals over which no one has any control. As with so many national enterprises, all Brantwood's American business ceased abruptly when the events of 9/11 rocked the world, just when the threat of foot and mouth disease had been reduced. Fortunately the economic downturn that began in 2009 discouraged the usual high numbers of British holidaymakers from flying abroad and boosted the numbers of visitors to attractions throughout the UK.

HILL TOP

'Her symphony and song'

Hill Top in Near Sawrey, Hawkshead, is a seventeenth-century farmhouse immortalized in words and pictures by the Edwardian writer Beatrix Potter, who wrote many of her children's stories here. Hill Top was as pivotal to Beatrix Potter's life as Dove Cottage was to Wordsworth's: six of her books are located in and around Hill Top. Owned by the National Trust and opened to visitors in 1944, it is now one of the most visited houses in Lakeland.

Beatrix Potter fell in thrall to the Lake District at the age of sixteen when, after many summers renting houses in Scotland, the Potter family changed its allegiance to the Lake District and rented the colossal Wray Castle (see page 180) for three months in 1882. *The Tale of Peter Rabbit*, privately published in 1901, was an instant sell-out and helped her to secure a contract with a London

publisher. She signed a contract in June 1902 and Frederick Warne agreed to print 8,000 copies, which were sold out before publication that October. Her royalties from Peter Rabbit and her early books gave her the opportunity to break away from her rather controlling parents in London and buy her first home. Inevitably it was in the Lake District and she planned to buy a small farm called Hill Top.

However, she had a rocky road ahead of her before all this could happen. She had fallen in love with Frederick Warne's son, Norman, and in spite of her parents' protestations they were engaged to be married on 25 July 1905. Beatrix was thirty-nine, Norman two years younger. Exactly a month later on 25 August, Norman was dead. He had succumbed to leukaemia and his end was swift.

In spite of these appalling circumstances Beatrix had only one door open to her: to continue with the purchase of Hill Top, a working farm of 14 hectares/34 acres with a typical seventeenth-century Lakeland farmhouse, with rendered stone walls and a Westmorland green slate roof. She acquired it in the autumn of 1905.

Beatrix immediately decided to build an extension to house her farm manager. This is the wing jutting out on the west side, which is still tenanted. She lived on and off at Hill Top from 1905 until 1913. Eight years later, upon her marriage to William Heelis, a local solicitor with an office in Hawkshead, Hill Top was obviously too small and as she was loath to add a further extension they chose to live at the larger Castle Farm nearby. Castle Farm remained her home until her death in December 1943. It can be seen from Hill Top and is permanently let to a local family, in accordance with her wishes.

Fortunately Beatrix Potter could afford to retain the cottage for the rest of her life. With no children of her own, the success of her books allowed her to buy fourteen more farms and thousands of acres of prime Lakeland pasture and fell. At the time of her death she had become one of the greatest conservators of the Lake District and she bequeathed all her property of 1,619 hectares/4,000 acres to the National Trust. This includes the famous beauty spot Tarn Hows, several farms and various cottages. She was also a highly successful farmer, famously breeding prize pigs and Herdwick sheep.

Since her death Hill Top has gradually become something of a shrine for lovers of her work from all over the world, notably the Japanese. Nowadays thousands of visitors a year make the pilgrimage to pay homage to Beatrix Potter and her much-loved characters and to track down the locations in her illustrations. Beatrix Potter was at pains to make sure that the interiors at Hill Top 'should be kept in their present condition'. She left precise details of where each item should stand, including her best pieces to be moved there from her married home of Castle Farm. Consequently, most of what we see today is still in the places she stipulated. Many of the scenes from her books can be recognized today just as she illustrated them. Yet the potential museum effect never works against Hill Top: the house is so homely that it feels as if the writer might be in the garden or she has strolled into the village of Near Sawrey. The house also acts as a social record of turn-of-the-century genteel country living in the Lake District, offering an idealized insight into how a domestic farmhouse may have been furnished and how a nineteenth-century farmer would have lived until the early years of the twentieth century.

Hill Top has a simple floor plan with two rooms to view downstairs: you come straight into the kitchen or entrance hall from the garden without any preliminary. The effect of recognizing details from her books is almost unnerving. Here is the stone-flagged floor, the range with gleaming horse brasses, the spinning wheel, there the oak long-case clock featured in *The Tailor of Gloucester*, to the right of the dresser.

The two teapot stands on the dresser were drawn by Beatrix as a girl. Above the oak press cupboard opposite the fireplace is a set of transfer-printed plates in blue, originally drawn by her father, Rupert Potter. Beatrix had the original range removed but the National Trust has filled in the wider opening with a larger range, better proportioned for the space available. If you look closely on the floor to the left of the dresser by the clock, you will discover the tiny hole used by Samuel Whiskers; his other escape route is close to the banisters on the landing. It is said that Beatrix had ninety-six rats killed. The wallpaper of 1906 had to be replaced with a screen-printed copy in 1987, covering the ceiling as well as the walls in the exuberant style beloved of the French. This was the room used to conduct farming business.

In the snug pine-panelled parlour on the right-hand side adjacent there is a triumph of overscaling with a white marble Adam-style chimneypiece, selected by Beatrix Potter herself. Reaching two-thirds of the height of the wall (the ceiling seems to hover close above one's head), and almost broad enough to touch the corner cupboard, it was surely meant for a spacious Edwardian salon rather than a diminutive Lakeland farmhouse. The rest of the room feels delightfully late Victorian, with a clutter of small paintings, books and china, Staffordshire greyhounds, decorative plates and miniatures. The hanging of the Potter family's coat of arms strikes a manorial note, as do the quirky door knockers, probably bought at auction, which do not look quite at home on an internal door.

Beatrix Potter's study on the first floor is still known as the 'new room', for it belongs to the extension she had built in 1906. With its position to the rear of the house on the first floor she was guaranteed light and peace; she wrote in the cool even light offered by the window. It is also one of the most personal rooms, not only created by her but used by her, worked on by her husband, who created the neo-classical panelling, and filled with the striking paintings of Scottish scenes by her brother, Bertram. He was influenced by John Everett Millais, who was a friend of the family and was a close neighbour of the Potter family in Bolton Gardens, London.

Husbands today are still accused of leaving DIY tasks uncompleted and William Heelis's unfinished carving over the door shows that little has changed in a century. Adjacent you will see three of the family's works of art: the top one a cartoon by her father, the middle one a study of trees by her mother and, below, one of Beatrix's illustrations, which is changed annually. She came from an artistic family and it is easy to understand how she developed her talents.

The Georgian, Victorian and Edwardian furniture lends an air of the quiet prosperity to be expected from a successful author. A copy of her first, most famous picture letter of 4 September 1893 to Noel Moore, her governess's first-born, signifies the birth of Peter Rabbit. Her assured and confident drawings of the 'four little rabbits' belie her uncertain beginning: 'I don't know what to say to you, so I shall tell you a story . . .' There is also a copy of a letter she received from *Country Life* magazine in 1913, rejecting three stories but accepting one.

Her bedroom is dominated by a seventeenth-century four-poster bed, with the pelmet embroidered by her while convalescing in her sixties. The William Morris design wallpaper is original.

BELOW Beatrix Potter's bedroom, with its original William Morris wallpaper.
RIGHT ABOVE The parlour and its overscaled Adam-style fireplace.
RIGHT BELOW The bottom shelf of this cupboard displays some of the earliest merchandise. Beatrix Potter was quick to realize the marketing potential of her books.

You approach Hill Top along a slate path bisecting double cottage garden borders that lead directly to the house. The garden is kept in the style favoured by Beatrix Potter, with a mixture of cottage garden flowers and herbs, fruit and vegetables. The positioning of the path allows you to feel surrounded by the plants and to see her much-loved cottage garden perennials in a seemingly artless arrangement. Her favourites included foxgloves, roses, lilies and phlox; others have been chosen as they are known to have been grown in her time. To strengthen the feel of an old-fashioned cottage garden the plants are grown in a delightfully random and haphazard way, spilling over the edges.

As with the interiors, the layout of the garden has altered little from the illustrations in the books. Opposite the front door a gate beckons you towards the kitchen garden, where in *The Tale of Peter Rabbit* Beatrix Potter imagined Mr McGregor's lettuces struggling against an onslaught of rabbits.

The Tale of Tom Kitten is a good indicator of her style of planting in her garden at Castle Farm. Using that book as a reference, along with surviving photographs, letters and local residents' memories, has defined how the garden at Hill Top looks today.

Hill Top is so popular that it has no worries about maintaining its high volume of visitors. With its premier position along with Dove Cottage as one of the best loved houses in the Lake District, publicity for Hill Top is correspondingly low key. There are no brown tourist signs and the National Trust's role is to ensure that visitors enjoy the house in the spirit that Beatrix Potter envisaged. This involves trying to retain the atmosphere of a small farmhouse

The approach to Hill Top is lined with cottage garden perennials.

17TH C The cottage is built.

28 July 1866 Birth of Beatrix Potter.

1882 When Beatrix is sixteen, after a decade of holidays in Scotland, her father, Rupert Potter, takes the mock-Norman Wray Castle on Windermere as a holiday home for the summer. This is her first link with the area. She meets Canon Rawnsley, who will become a founder member of the National Trust when it is formed in 1895, with her father as one of the first life members.

1885 Beatrix's governess, Annie Carter, marries Edwin Moore.

1887 Their son, Noel Moore, is born.

1893 Beatrix's picture letter to Noel will transform her life: Peter Rabbit is born. A steady flow of letters encourages Annie to turn Beatrix's thoughts to publication.

1901 After several rejections from publishers Beatrix self-publishes 250 copies of *The Tale of Peter Rabbit* for the Christmas market.

1902 She signs a contract with F. Warne to publish 8,000 copies and develops a close working relationship with Norman Warne, agreeing to produce two books per year.

1903 She buys a field in Near Sawrey. *Peter Rabbit* has sold 50,000 copies.

25 July 1905 She accepts a written proposal of marriage from Norman in spite of her parents' fierce opposition.

25 August 1905 Norman has become gravely ill with leukemia and dies. Beatrix determines to make a fresh start.

Autumn 1905 She goes through with the already planned purchase of Hill Top Farm and 34 acres, buildings and orchard for £2,805 with the profits of her first published books, only to discover later that she has paid over the odds. Although she is living primarily in London, Hill Top becomes her Lakeland home.

1906 Retaining the farm manager John Cannon and his family, she has an extension built. She uses Hill Top as a studio, writing in the new room.

1908 W.H. Heelis & Son become her solicitors as a respected children's author she has enough money to buy land and increase livestock. William Heelis becomes her property manager, friend and companion.

1909 She purchases Castle Farm in Near Sawrey along with 10 hectares/25 acres adjoining Hill Top Farm.

1912 When Beatrix is almost forty-seven, William proposes but her parents oppose the marriage. The strain shows and she contracts bronchial pneumonia, which weakens her heart. After learning that their son, Bertram, has been secretly married for over a decade, her parents relent.

15 October 1913 Beatrix becomes Mrs William Heelis.

May 1914 Her father dies of stomach cancer, while Beatrix is in London. She moves her mother to Lindeth Howe, Windermere, already used by the family as a holiday home.

1914 Castle Farm becomes the Heelis's new home at the end of year.

1918 Her brother, Bertram Potter, dies, aged 46.

1920 Death of Canon Rawnsley from whom Beatrix learned the need to fight for and preserve the countryside.

1923 She purchases Troutbeck Park Farm and 2,000 acres.

1928 To stave off developers encroaching on Cockshott Point on Windermere's foreshore, Beatrix creates coloured drawings, many of which are snapped up in America, and the land is saved.

1930 She purchases the Monk Coniston estate, stretching from Little Langdale to Coniston and including Tarn Hows. She offers half of the estate at cost to the National Trust. Once the sale is agreed, she manages the entire estate.

1932 Death of Beatrix Potter's mother, aged ninety-three.

1934 In spite of her publisher's demands, she feels 'written out'.

1939 She recovers from a major operation.

December 1943 Beatrix dies after bronchitis and heart trouble.

1944 The National Trust becomes the owner of Hill Top and it opens to the public.

1945 William Heelis dies, having not long survived without his wife.

and allowing visitors to enjoy what they have come to view, without feeling too controlled or squeezed in. The National Trust's aim, as ever, is to preserve the house and its contents for future generations, yet the sheer weight of numbers – many more encouraged by the film *Miss Potter*, starring Renée Zellweger – has meant that the trust has had to institute a timed ticket operation, with early sell-outs almost guaranteed in school holidays.

Any activities that can involve the garden, where space is not at such a premium, have been seized upon. One such activity is the monthly cottage garden weekends, at which the mysteries of planting and the joy of growing plants are unfolded for children, and recipes using seasonal produce are highlighted. The Beatrix Potter Gallery in the nearby village of Hawkshead also absorbs visitors' time. While they are waiting to view Hill Top, time can be well spent getting a flavour of the writer and her creations.

The high pressure on properties such as Hill Top in their possession has given the National Trust environmental concerns regarding the number of visitors motoring to their properties and it encourages them to find an alternative to their vehicles. Hill Top's car park fills up alarmingly fast, so the trust also suggests parking at Ash Landing or Harrowslack and approaching via the fields. The narrow winding lanes south of Ambleside become easily congested at weekends and busy times, so the trust is keen to point out that it is only a 3-kilometre/2-mile walk from the reasonably priced Windermere ferry. The Lake District's specialist minibus tours and cycling are other options.

To guard against having to turn away too many disappointed families, Hill Top has recently extended its hours by opening an hour earlier in the morning. The trust also encourages visitors to view other attractions associated with and bequeathed by Beatrix Potter, such as Tarn Hows and Monk Coniston, to relieve some of the pressure on Hill Top.

VICTORIAN
HOUSES

WRAY CASTLE

Grandiose Wray Castle was built in the 1840s on the western shore of Windermere. It is the largest private building in the Sawrey area near Hawkshead; and as an early nineteenth-century castellated mansion it is unique in the county. Indeed, few houses in this style exist in the rest of Britain. It is contemporary with Conishead Priory (see page 74), and resembles Penrhyn Castle, built between 1820 and 1845, Thomas Hopper's neo-Norman fantasy castle in Snowdonia, created for the Pennant family.

Wray Castle and its location had an enormous effect on two protagonists involved in the early years of the National Trust: one of its founders, Canon Hardwicke Drummond Rawnsley, and its major Lakeland benefactor, Beatrix Potter.

Back in 1836, the Liverpool surgeon Dr James Dawson and his wife Margaret, who had inherited the Preston family's distillery fortune, were gradually extending their estate on Windermere's western shore to 336 hectares/830 acres. The estate included a villa known as Wray Cottage, where they lived for some years before demolishing it to make way for an exciting new project.

Various heraldic panels indicate that the Dawsons began to build Wray Castle around 1840. The 'castle' was designed by a little-known Liverpool architect, John Jackson Lightfoot, who died prematurely from drink in 1843, and is considered to be his one and only major commission. Echoes of the young Philip Wyatt's chequered career at Conishead Priory are difficult to ignore.

By 1846 the gothic revival castle appears to have been completed, built in brooding dressed slate with grey limestone quoins. In order to make a significant impression from the opposite shore, it rises as something of a Colossus, only 200 metres/656 feet from the shoreline, and today revealing its castellations above the tree canopy. What it lacks in lightness of touch it compensates for with an extravagance of irregular crenellated towers and turrets, which are rather fun.

PREVIOUS PAGES Looking up to the first-floor landing and the tower at Wray Castle.
LEFT The castle stands like a Colossus on Windermere's western shore.

Whatever the effect the Dawsons were striving for, Wray is a fantasy castle, much more angular but somewhat reminiscent of King Ludwig of Bavaria's Neuschwanstein and Walt Disney's fairytale castle. The approach reveals a mighty *porte cochère* (covered porch), large enough to accommodate a billiard room above, attached to the main block of reception rooms and bedrooms. There is also a smaller servants' wing.

The interior is also in the gothic style, with elaborate mouldings. The triple sequence of halls – entrance hall, central hall and stair hall – soaring through three floors to the central tower is its most memorable feature, and the most profligate use of space imaginable. The library, drawing room, dining room, morning room and music room are all fabulous rooms, with hefty skirtings and massive doors. These last two rooms are the best preserved, having retained their surviving chimneypieces.

After Margaret Dawson died in 1862, followed by James in 1875, aged ninety-five, the estate passed to her relatives. This was a pivotal moment for Wray Castle, leading eventually to the National Trust assuming ownership in 1929. The seeds were sown by Canon Rawnsley.

Canon Rawnsley was appointed to the living of Low Wray in 1877 after his cousin, Edward Preston Rawnsley, became the chief beneficiary of the Dawsons' estate as a minor of fourteen years. When Beatrix Potter's father, Rupert, took a summer rental on Wray Castle in 1882 the sixteen-year-old Beatrix was alerted to the unique qualities of the surroundings, which led to

The exuberant ceiling in the music room has recently been restored.

her lifelong passion for the Sawrey area, where she would eventually settle (see page 171). Her friendship with Rawnsley began that summer also, before he left for Crosthwaite near Keswick after five years, becoming an honorary Canon of Carlisle Cathedral in 1891.

By 1898 Edward Rawnsley decided to sell the Wray Castle estate to David Ainsworth, a West Cumberland industrialist and Member of Parliament for Westmorland, who also knew the property well, having rented it since 1882. After his death in 1907 his wife remained there until 1920. The estate then had a variety of owners until 1928.

Fortunately in the following year Sir Noton Barclay, a former Lord Mayor of Manchester, stepped in and was able to offer the core of the estate, the castle and 26 hectares/64 acres, to the National Trust. Beatrix Potter and her husband, William Heelis, acquired certain farms on the estate at the same time, which eventually passed to the National Trust on their deaths.

In the late 1920s, anything Victorian was still out of fashion, and securing this stretch of lake frontage and the land was regarded as far more important than the buildings. The castle had undergone very few alterations since Dr James Dawson had died half a century before, the most notable being improvements to windows in the servants' wing in an attempt to provide more light. Wray Castle continued to be preserved in aspic during the following years, as the National Trust let it to a number of institutional tenants from 1931 to 2004. Negotiations to transform Wray Castle into a luxury hotel have been ongoing since 2004.

A view from the castle northwards, overlooking Windermere.

LANGDALE CHASE

A cross the lake from Wray Castle and commanding an elevated location above the north-eastern shore of Windermere between Ambleside and the town of Windermere lies Langdale Chase, now a hotel. It takes its name from the Langdale Pikes, which are central to the panorama on the opposite side of the lake. Wordsworth described this location as 'the loveliest spot that man hath ever found', although whether he would have welcomed the erection of yet another 1890s villa in a prominent location on Windermere's shore is open to speculation. Few house locations in the Lake District are as good: the world-class view is heart-stopping.

In 1890 Mr Howarth, a Manchester businessman, was able to purchase the site, hoping to build a small retreat for himself and his wife amid 1.8 hectares/4½ acres bursting with potential. However, his early death cancelled their plans and his widow, Mrs Edna Howarth, forged ahead with a more grandiose scheme, with a view to making this place her permanent home. The architects Mrs Howarth commissioned were J.L. Ball, J.T. Lee and Pattinson of Manchester, and her only daughter, Lily, laid the foundation stone on 8 April 1890. Five years later the house was completed, with the distinction of being the first house in Windermere to be wired for electricity.

In many ways Langdale Chase, built of Brathay Blue stone for the enormous sum of £32,000, is similar to those grand Victorian buildings which have survived in the centres of Manchester, Leeds and Liverpool. The style is Victorian Jacobethan and somewhat reminiscent of Holker Hall (see page 102). An irregular assortment of gables topped with stone balls, soaring chimneys and an impressive cupola crowning a triple-storey corner window creates an opulent effect. Inside, armorial stained glass and ornate ceilings are key features. The

Langdale Chase enjoys one of the Lake District's most strategic locations, on Windermere's eastern shore.

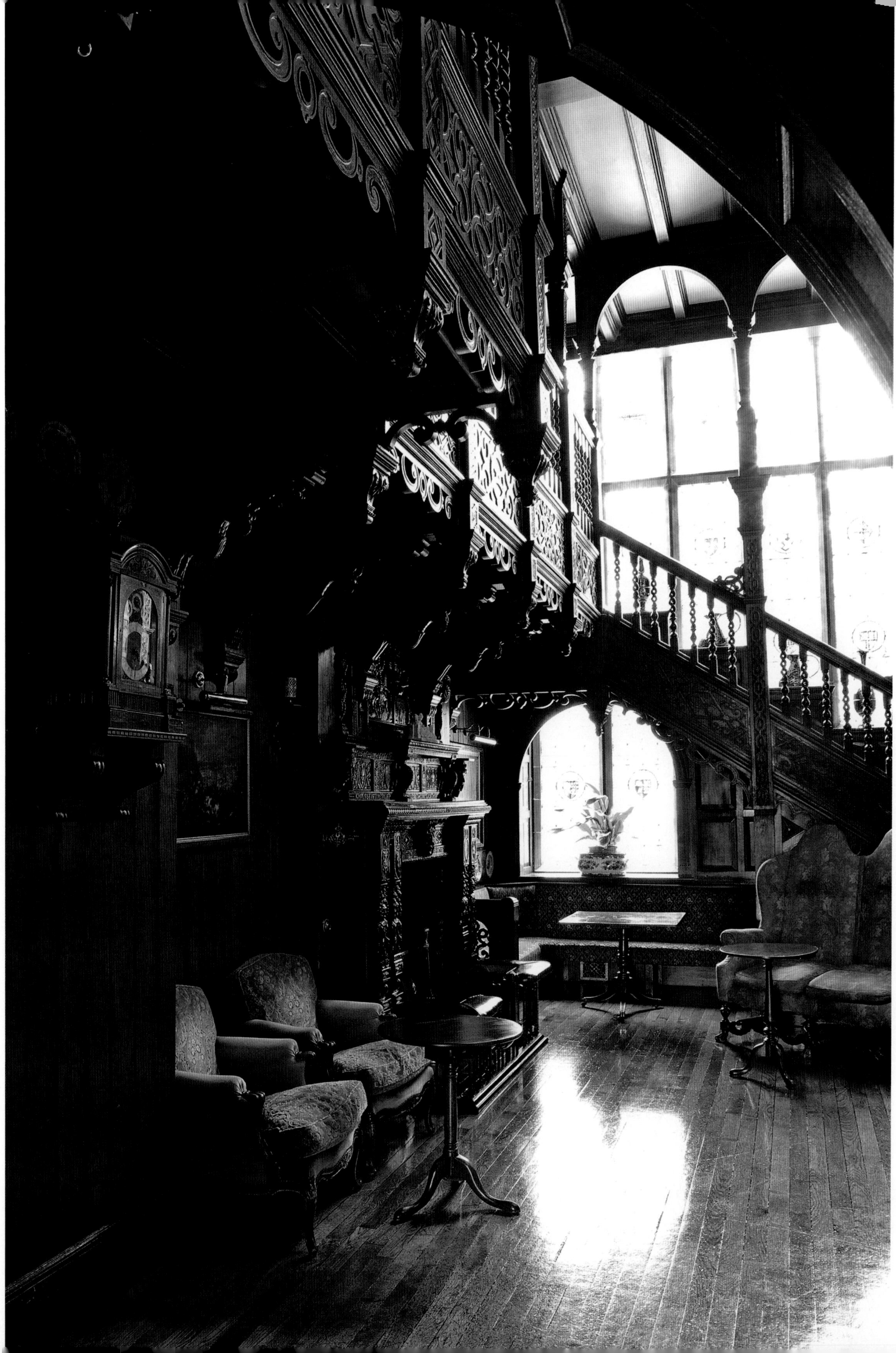

soaring main hall is a tour de force of panelling, balconies and richly carved oak. In 1896 Mrs Howarth had one of the finest boathouses on the lake built in the same style and ordered a 15-metre/50-foot teak launch, *Lily*, all plush velvet and leather, from Brockbank of Bowness; renamed *Branksome*, it can be seen in the Windermere steamboat museum.

Mrs Howarth continued to reside here until her death in 1914, that pivotal year that saw so many changes to society. With her wealth she was able to spend her last years enjoying the kind of comfortable and well-established Edwardian routine unimaginable today, with eight indoor servants and a further eight responsible for the carriages, boats and gardens. A constant round of garden parties, croquet and tennis punctuated the summer months, until the world began to alter for ever with the outbreak of the First World War.

Although 1914 was a catastrophic year on the world stage, it was kinder to Langdale Chase. Upon the sale of the property, Mr and Mrs Willows from Scarborough relocated to Langdale Chase to avoid the anticipated shelling on the east coast, bringing with them a horde of treasures. The hall still exhibits their collection of paintings, china plates and oak, which all conspire to create the atmosphere of an old world mansion. The oak fireplace, dated 1664, has a local connection. It is inscribed with the name 'Elizabeth, Countess of Thanet', who was the daughter of Lady Anne Clifford, an indomitable lady in the old county of Westmorland. Lady Anne Clifford inherited castles in Appleby, Brough, Brougham, Pendragon and Skipton upon the death of her uncle, the Earl of Cumberland, in 1643, and made it her life's work to restore them. This fireplace would have been salvaged from one of those castles. The dining room has early Tudor panelling brought by Mr Willows from a London house.

The Willowses enjoyed a good fifteen years here, ending in 1929 with the death of Mrs Willows, a few years after that of her husband. However, the years of baronial leisured living were finally drawing to a close. An auction of Langdale Chase failed to secure a bid and three weeks later Miss Dorothy Dalzell, along with her mother and aunt, purchased the property and ran it as a hotel, while retaining the aura of a country house. They welcomed their first guests in the Easter of 1930. When the dining room was extended in 1950, Langdale Chase claimed another first with revolutionary large windows, realizing the full potential of the panorama.

Langdale Chase continued to be something of a repository for genuine bits and pieces from old houses, in the manner of Hearst Castle, California, the ostentatious mansion of the newspaper magnate Randolph Hearst. The large window to the left of the front door dates back to 1900, and came from Grizedale Hall, demolished in 1955. The internationally known local landscape architect Thomas Mawson was commissioned to design the garden and it is one of his finest, making sense of the change of levels. The glitzy film-set aura of the house and setting owes much to his elegant stone balustrade, which encloses the terraces leading out from the French windows towards that unforgettable view.

After more than forty years in February 1974 Miss Dalzell sold Langdale Chase to Mr and Mrs Buckley. He died in November of that year and his widow stayed there until her death in 1981. The Schaefer and Noblett families are the current owners and take great pride in following the traditions established by the varied previous occupants.

PREVIOUS PAGES Like the rest of the house, the hall is in late Victorian Jacobethan style. The oak fireplace (left) dates from 1664. A minstrel's gallery (right) looks on to the hall, and Old Master paintings embellish the country-house style.

RIGHT ABOVE AND BELOW The garden descends to Windermere. The steps and balustrades were designed by Thomas Mawson.

BROAD LEYS

Broad Leys was built in 1898 and designed by C.F.A. Voysey (1857–1941) for Mr A.C. Briggs of Leeds. Located just south of Bowness, it is considered by the architectural historian Sir Nikolaus Pevsner to be his masterpiece. He was a contemporary of Hugh Baillie Scott, the architect of nearby Blackwell (see page 114).

Charles Voysey was a Yorkshireman and began his career designing wallpapers, fabrics and furnishings. He was influenced by the work of A.W.N. Pugin (who designed the interiors and furniture for the new Houses of Parliament in the 1840s) and inspired by the English vernacular sources of the sixteenth and early seventeenth centuries. Voysey is revered today for his minimalist and spacious look, favouring straight lines and moderate curves. His style is similar to that of Charles Rennie Mackintosh (1868–1928), the influential Glaswegian architect who designed in the Arts and Crafts style and was Britain's leading exponent of Art Nouveau. Voysey also employed a Lakeland vernacular farmhouse style with white roughcast walls, chimney stacks and a sweeping Westmorland green slate roof. The typically ornate and intricate design, fashionable in the 1890s, as seen at Langdale Chase (see page 184) was abhorrent to him.

The most striking external feature at Broad Leys is the linked trio of triple-storey curved bow windows, which seem to fill the entire west elevation, soaring from the ground to the hipped roof. They maximize the views of Windermere and the western fells, and bring light to the spacious interiors. In 1951 the Windermere Motor Boat Racing Club acquired the property and it has been its clubhouse ever since. It is the only Voysey house in the world offering accommodation to paying guests. Since the Lake District Planning Board imposed a 10mph speed limit for boats on Windermere in 2005, the club now races in Barrow docks.

LEFT Broad Leys, C.F.A. Voysey's masterpiece.

FOLLOWING PAGES The house's Elizabethan-style windows look over Windermere towards the western fells.

NETHERWOOD

Located in one of Cumbria's mildest locations in Grange-over-Sands, an area formerly known as Lancashire north-of-the-sands, lies the Netherwood Hotel, completed in 1893. It enjoys a splendid view of the wide expanse of Morecambe Bay, described by Wordsworth as 'the majestic plain where the sea has retired'. Netherwood was built as a private house for George W. Deakin, a wealthy cotton merchant from Bolton, and his wife, Maude.

Deakin originally purchased a late Georgian house on the site called Blawith Cottage, which he had demolished. In its place he created the house of today (then known as Blawith), built in the Jacobean style in local limestone with sandstone mullioned and transomed windows. The architects were Messrs Willink and Thickness of Liverpool, who began their practice in 1884 and ended it in 1920 upon the death of Thickness. William Willink (b. 1856) was articled to Alfred Waterhouse and Philip Thickness (1860–1920) to Norman Shaw, who was involved with the Albert Hall Mansions in Kensington, London. They worked on the extension to the Liverpool School of Art in 1910 and several ship interiors.

Netherwood has similarities to Levens Hall (see page 34). Its crenellated bold square tower echoes the familiar Cumbrian pele tower. Irregular steep gables and obelisks add vigour to the front elevation and the familiar crop of Westmorland cylindrical chimneys lend an air of confidence. Splendid greenhouses adjacent to the main building, now demolished, used to supply the family with fresh fruit and vegetables. The house looks grand and wide, but to all intents and purposes it is one pile (row) of rooms deep, largely because it is set back to within a few feet of the fell and woodland – descriptively known as Paradise Hill – rising behind. However, the shallow design affords every reception room a fine view of Morecambe Bay.

Netherwood's square tower, irregular gables, round Westmorland chimneys and mullioned windows are in the style of Levens Hall. The 1990s extension does not jar.

The interiors are thought to be by Gillows of Lancaster. The leaded-light windows are busy with armorial stained and painted glass. The elaborate plaster ceilings, oak panelling and ornate carving in many of the rooms were surely influenced by Sizergh and Levens (see pages 22 and 34), and the ballroom in particular has an outstandingly ornate barrel plaster ceiling with interlocking quatrefoils.

Sadly George Deakin had only four years to enjoy his new property, dying in April 1897, leaving Maude to continue living there until her death in the late 1920s. The house then stood empty until in 1935 a Captain Silas purchased it and began to run it as a hotel – a familiar story. After his own house, called Netherwood, had burned down he changed the name from Blawith to Netherwood. His time was brief and Miss Chalmers and Miss Lawrence took up the reins in the late 1930s. When the Second World War broke out in 1939 they had to house evacuees and billet troops.

After the war the two women sold the property to a group of businessmen, who unfortunately did not appreciate the running costs required to keep such a building in good order and began to asset-strip. The glasshouses were demolished and cheap chalet-style properties mushroomed in their place. Netherwood had reached a nadir, but in 1966 it was purchased and saved by the Fallowfield family, who continue to personally run the hotel on traditional lines. Netherwood is a charismatic and much-loved building that has no trouble in finding admirers today. Its character, the superb quality of its craftsmanship and its commanding setting have made it a highly sought-after wedding venue.

RIGHT ABOVE The manorial entrance hall.
RIGHT BELOW A built-in dresser and linenfold panelling in the former dining room.
FAR RIGHT, ABOVE The bar, formerly the dining room, has a net-like ceiling in the style of Serlio.
FAR RIGHT, BELOW In the drawing room the five-panelled framing is similar to that in Sizergh Castle's inlaid chamber, while the plasterwork echoes Sizergh's Elizabethan ceilings.

ARMATHWAITE HALL

Armathwaite Hall in the north of the county overlooks Bassenthwaite Lake and has associations with James Spedding, whose family would come to own Mirehouse (see page 151), and the Fletcher Vane family of Hutton-in-the-Forest (see page 80). This location has been the site of a hall since the eleventh century. James Spedding and three generations of his family owned the hall from 1748 until he sold it to Sir Frederick Fletcher Vane in 1796. In 1817 the family made certain alterations and additions, extending towards the lake and building a chapel and new courtyard. In 1850, four generations of the Fletcher Vanes later, a Mr Boustead, whose family had made a fortune in tea in Ceylon, purchased the hall.

The present building has emerged from a remodelling by a local mine owner, Thomas Hartley, who bought Armathwaite from Mr Boustead for the huge sum of £95,000 in 1880 and had the wherewithal to put the stamp of a country gentleman's residence on it. He was able to enjoy almost fifty years there, being fortunate to live until 1926. He built on what are now the hall, lounge, lake room and cocktail bar. On his death the estate was sold in lots, but the hall and its surrounding 54 hectares/133 acres proved unsaleable. Just as the threat of auction for demolition was casting its long shadow, the owners of the Keswick Hotel, the Wivells, purchased the hall and its land for £5,000. After six months of renovations they opened the doors to hotel guests. Armathwaite Hall continues to be run as a hotel to this day, with a break in the Second World War to accommodate the evacuated Hunmanby Hall Girls School.

Today's owners, the Graves family, purchased the hotel from the Wivells in 1976 and have worked hard to ensure its place as one of the Lake District's most luxurious hotels.

PREVIOUS PAGES The hall looks out over Bassenthwaite Lake to Sale Fell and Ling Fell.

LEFT The baronial hall.

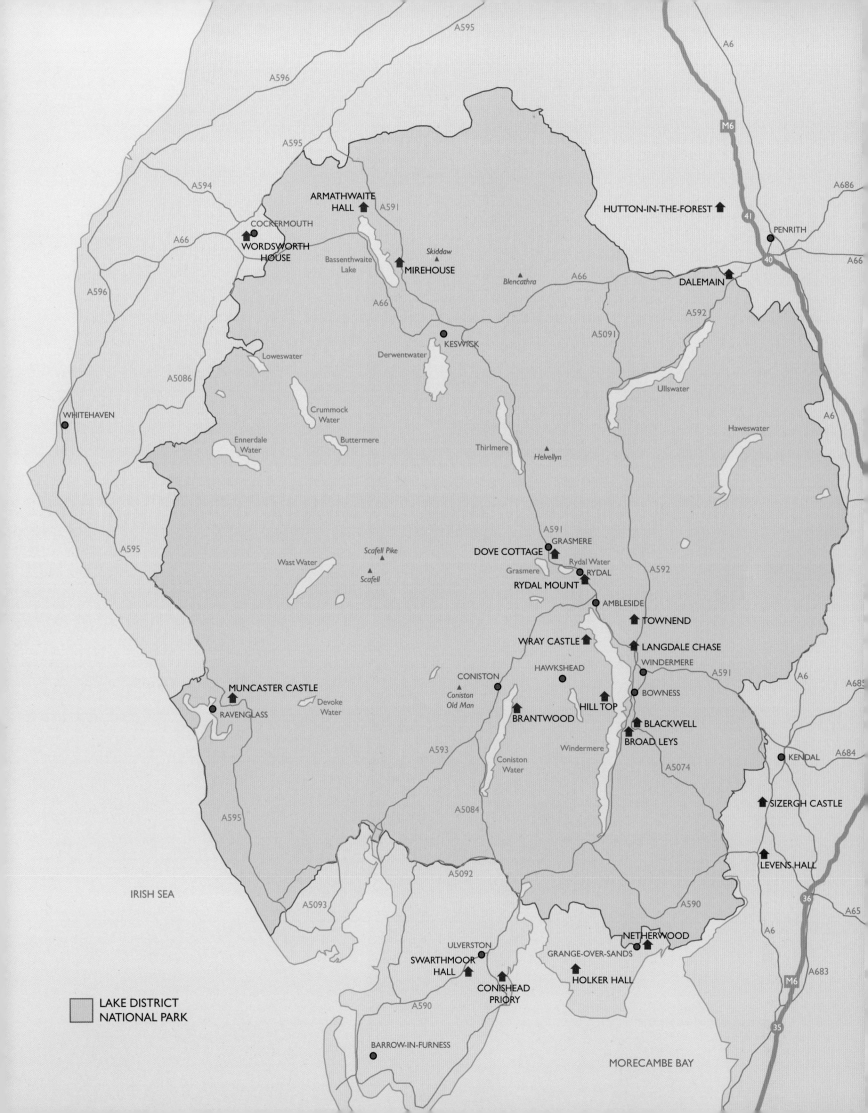

A595

A596

A6

A595

A596

A594

A66

COCKERMOUTH

**WORDSWORTH
HOUSE**

ARMATHWAITE
HALL

A591

Skiddaw

MIREHOUSE

Bassenthwaite
Lake

Blencathra

A66

HUTTON-IN-THE-FOREST

41

PENRITH

40

A6

A66

A686

DALEMAIN

A592

A5091

A5086

Loweswater

Derwentwater

KESWICK

Ullswater

WHITEHAVEN

Crummock
Water

Buttermere

Haweswater

Ennerdale
Water

Thirlmere

Helvellyn

A6

A595

Scafell Pike

Wast Water

Scafell

A591

GRASMERE

DOVE COTTAGE

Grasmere

Rydal Water

RYDAL

A592

RYDAL MOUNT

AMBLESIDE

TOWNEND

WRAY CASTLE

LANGDALE CHASE

WINDERMERE

A591

A6

A685

MUNCASTER CASTLE

CONISTON

HAWKSHEAD

*Coniston
Old Man*

BOWNESS

HILL TOP

RAVENGLASS

Devoke
Water

BRANTWOOD

BLACKWELL

BROAD LEYS

Windermere

KENDAL

A684

A593

Coniston
Water

A5074

A5084

SIZERGH CASTLE

LEVENS HALL

A595

A5092

36

IRISH SEA

A5093

A590

A6

A65

NETHERWOOD

ULVERSTON

GRANGE-OVER-SANDS

**SWARTHMOOR
HALL**

HOLKER HALL

**CONISHEAD
PRIORY**

A590

M6

A683

35

BARROW-IN-FURNESS

MORECAMBE BAY

**LAKE DISTRICT
NATIONAL PARK**

VISITOR INFORMATION

HOUSES OPEN TO THE PUBLIC

Blackwell, The Arts & Crafts House
Bowness-on-Windermere
Cumbria
LA23 3JT
015394 46139
www.blackwell.org.uk

The Brantwood Trust
Coniston
Cumbria
LA21 8AD
015394 41396
www.brantwood.org.uk

Conishead Priory
Manjushri Kadampa Meditation Centre
Ulverston
LA12 9QQ
01229 584029
www.conisheadpriory.org

Dalemain
Penrith
CA11 OHB
017684 86450
www.dalemain.com

Dove Cottage
The Wordsworth Museum & Art Gallery
Grasmere
LA22 9SH
015394 35544
www.wordsworth.org.uk

Hill Top
Near Sawrey
Ambleside
LA22 0LF
015394 36269
www.nationaltrust.org.uk

Holker Hall
Cark-in-Cartmel
Nr Grange-over-Sands
LA11 7PL
015395 58328
www.holker.co.uk

Hutton-in-the-Forest
Penrith
CA11 9TH
017684 84449
www.hutton-in-the-forest.co.uk

Levens Hall
Kendal
LA8 0PD
015395 60321
www.levenshall.co.uk

Mirehouse
Keswick
CA12 4QE
017687 72287
www.mirehouse.com

Muncaster Castle
Ravenglass
CA18 1RQ
01229 717614
www.muncaster.co.uk

Rydal Mount
Rydal
Ambleside
LA22 9LU
015394 33002
www.rydalmount.co.uk

Sizergh Castle
Sizergh
Nr Kendal
LA8 8AE
015395 60581
www.nationaltrust.org.uk

Swarthmoor Hall
Ulverston
LA12 0JQ
01229 583204
www.swarthmoorhall.co.uk

Townend
Troutbeck
Windermere
LA23 1LB
015394 32628
www.nationaltrust.org.uk

Wordsworth House
Main Street
Cockermouth
CA13 9RX
01900 820884
www.nationaltrust.org.uk

HOUSES CONVERTED INTO HOTELS OR HAVING OTHER USES

Armathwaite Hall
Bassenthwaite Lake
Keswick
CA12 4RE
017687 76551
www.armathwaite-hall.com

Broad Leys
Ghyll Head
Newby Bridge Road
Windermere
LA23 3LJ
015394 43284
www.wmbrc.co.uk

Langdale Chase Hotel
Ambleside Road
Windermere
LA23 1LW
015394 32201
www.langdalechase.co.uk

Netherwood Hotel
Lindale Road
Grange-over-Sands
LA11 6ET
015395 32552
www.netherwood-hotel.co.uk

Wray Castle
Claife
LA22 0JA
For further information, and details
of occasional public access, see
www.nationaltrust.org.uk

INDEX

Page numbers for illustrations and captions are given in **Bold**

RECOMMENDED FOR FURTHER READING

Beard, Geoffrey, *The Greater House in Cumbria*, Westmorland Gazette, 1978
Brunskill, R.W., *Traditional Buildings of Cumbria*, Yale University Press, 2010
Crowder, Chris, *The Garden at Levens*, Frances Lincoln, 2005
Davies, Hunter, *William Wordsworth*, Frances Lincoln, 2009
Hebron, Stephen, *Dove Cottage*, The Wordsworth Trust, 2009
Hyde, Matthew, and Pevsner, Nikolaus, *Cumbria: The Buildings of England*, Yale University Press, 2010
Jackson-Stops, Gervase, and Pipkin, James, *The English Country House: A Grand Tour*, Weidenfeld & Nicolson, 1993
Lindop, Grevel, *A Literary Guide to the Lake District*, Sigma Press, 2005
Wordsworth, Dorothy, *The Grasmere Journals*: various editions
Wordsworth, William, poems: various editions

I have chosen quotations from S.T. Coleridge's 'Kubla Khan' for the main chapters in recognition of his friendship with Wordsworth. The great diarist James Lees-Milne (1909–97) also quoted from that poem to create titles for his published diaries. In combination with my love of house visiting in Britain, those diaries have underpinned my background knowledge of a vanished world.

ACKNOWLEDGMENTS

AUTHOR'S ACKNOWLEDGMENTS

Most books have one author, but few authors can produce a book single-handed. I acknowledge with sincere thanks the help I have received from a number of people in the preparation of this book. In particular I am grateful to Clive Boursnell for taking on the daunting task of photographing so many exteriors, interiors, gardens and people in Cumbria. I should also like to thank the house owners and curators who agreed to be interviewed; William H.C. Wycherley, FRICS; Nicky Godfrey-Evans, Cumbria Blue Badge Guide. David Parker, on the home front, has attempted to distance himself, but this has not prevented him from making countless valuable suggestions. Thanks also to the team at Frances Lincoln.

I have done my best to ensure the accuracy of information in the book, but would be happy to correct errors, if any there be, in later editions.

PHOTOGRAPHER'S ACKNOWLEDGMENTS

Firstly, I say thank you to Christopher Holliday for asking if I would like to do the photography in one of the most glorious parts of the country, and for his kindly consideration for my workload, delicious suppers in good company and having the best bedroom view in England.

To my editor, Jo Christian, for her close and constant support, where no problem was off limits and her time never denied to me, thank you Jo.

To photograph a book like this one would be totally impossible to achieve with out the goodwill and active support of the house owners. The delight I felt when Mr Hal Bagot of Levens Hall (whose garden I have loved and photographed these last twenty years), on hearing that I was doing the photographs, was happy to leave me to get on with the work by myself, and I found this throughout my photographic house visits. The trust that was afforded to me I will always remember and deeply treasure.

To Lord and Lady Inglewood, of Hutton-in-the-Forest, for their very warm welcome and for including me into their daily household during my visits, and what an absolute joy to be in their garden as well as the house, a real favourite of mine.

To Jeanette Edgar and her team at Blackwell for the freedom to come and go and work as it suited me. It was the same with Stephen Cousin and Howard Hull of Brantwood.

To the National Trust for the open and kindly access they gave me to their properties, Hill Top, to Catherine Pritchard for her care, tea and biscuits in the garden at Hill Top, to Alex and her team at Cockermouth, to Emma and her team at Townend, to Margaret and Emma at Sizergh Castle and to Paul at Wray Castle.

Roy Tyson and all his loving people at Conishead Priory, and for clearing the cars in pouring rain. The peaceful simplicity of Swarthmoor Hall, and Rydal Mount with its tumbling garden down to water's edge.

To Robert and Jane Hasell-McCosh of Dalemain and her delightful elderly mother, for coping with my wants and for their daughter, Beatrice, who was a most wonderful assistant to me for a day, and to the entire household. I just love the blue poppies and marmalade, and I learned to cope with some dead wood.

To Janeki and James Spedding of Mirehouse, for a peaceful day's shoot and a good lunch on the run amongst the humbling literati of yesteryear. The tiny charming Dove Cottage, where I jollily worked squashed between wave after wave of Japanese tourists.

To the owners of the 'Great Victorian piles', now hotels, Armathwaite, Langdale Chase, Netherwood and the later boat club of Broad Ley, I say a big thank-you for your welcome, coffee and sandwiches. To Margaret of Tymparon Hall B&B for forgiving me for setting off the fire alarm at 5.30 in the morning while burning my toast.

Far flung to the west, Muncaster Castle, the extraordinary home of Mr and Mrs Frost-Pennington: I thank them for their most generous efforts to make everything work for me, including at a moment's notice giving me what must be one of the biggest double beds in England to sleep in, when my poor old camper bus broke down on the Hard Knott pass. It was David Benson of High Bridge End, Ulpha, who so kindly drove me off the moor to Muncaster Castle and, what is more, came back for me the following morning after my shooting, so that I could be back with my camper bus when AA patrolman Martyn King, with no fuss or ado, very quickly fixed on the spot the broken water cooling system. You're not forgotten; thank you.

To Lord and Lady Cavendish of Holker Hall, their most splendid home and gardens, to their lovely house ladies, and to Karen Seaman for her great help with my photography, after dark. Karen, you made the billiard room shot work – thanks. The discovery and delight of being in the garden for the first time was one of my high points of this project.

The making of this book has been truly a very great privilege for me. To be able, without hindrance, to immerse myself in the unique atmosphere of each property is something I will for ever hold dear. I thank you all very much indeed.

To Becky Clarke of Frances Lincoln, for her brilliant design sense, her sensitive eye to my work, and her ever constant support. Thank you, Becky.

Last but not least, Barbara Grant, my partner, who of course has had to put up with me returning home exhausted, like a grumpy old bear, only days later to joyfully go skipping off back to the Lakes, leaving her behind: I owe you one, or two, me love.